"Gary Burnett has an academic mind, a devotional heart, and a cultural perception. This unique blend gives him the ability to take big theological ideas and distill them into short, accessible teaching sessions. They are inspirational, insightful, and instructional. You will read the text afresh and hear the call to live it in challenging ways."

—STEVE STOCKMAN
Pastor, blogger, and author of *Walk On: The Spiritual Journey of U2*

"Is Paul past his sell-by date? This wonderful little book shows how relevant and important the apostle Paul's letters are in today's world. Gary Burnett writes in an engaging and unstuffy way, drawing on many years of study of Paul to shine light on Paul's major themes and ideas. Christians today will find this book engages them; illuminates their thinking, believing, and living; and challenges and provokes them to action in world and church. Bravo!"

—STEVE WALTON
Professor of New Testament, Trinity College, Bristol, United Kingdom

"In this gem Gary Burnett is inviting us to see beyond Paul, 'the theologian,' and offering a view of the trees in the forest of interpretations, providing us with an opportunity to engage the core of Paul's experience—keenly helping us to become *in essence* more meaningful theologians."

—RAYMOND CARR
Assistant Professor of Theology and Ethics, Pepperdine University

"I have loved Gary's latest book, *Paul Distilled*. Having listened to the original series I wondered could they be bettered, and they are! Gary captures the heart of Paul coupled with biblical accuracy and insights into the text while bringing practical challenge to his readers. This is a book which exudes with joy, life, and gives the reader a fresh desire to serve God with passion. I thoroughly recommend it to you."

—PAUL REID
Pastor Emeritus, Christian Fellowship Church, Belfast, Ireland

"As a master distiller, Gary Burnett builds on the foundational flavor of Paul's understanding of God's love before mixing in the more complex elements of Paul's theology, moderated with personal narratives. The result is a full-bodied, well-balanced, and very accessible book. *Paul Distilled* is an excellent introduction to Paul while providing wonderful flavor notes for the well-informed reader."

—NEIL CRAIGAN
Pastor, First Presbyterian Church, White Bear Lake, Minnesota

"*Paul Distilled* gives us access to the apostle in first-century Rome and makes connections to our world and faith in practical and powerful ways. References to song lyrics will make you smile and contemplate the true meaning of love."

—SARAH WHITTLE
Research Fellow in Biblical Studies, Nazarene Theological College

"'Contextualization' has become a buzzword in theological studies in recent years. Burnett skillfully considers how the original textual context should influence our interpretation of Pauline theology in the contexts in which we find ourselves today. Drawing on his years of study and teaching, Burnett sums up the 'essence of Paul' in a way that is accessible to those who simply wish to deepen their knowledge, and thought-provoking for those undertaking Pauline studies. I will be recommending it for years to come."

—JANET UNSWORTH
Director of Theological Education and Principal, Edgehill Theological College

Paul Distilled

Paul Distilled

GARY W. BURNETT

WIPF & STOCK · Eugene, Oregon

PAUL DISTILLED

Wipf & Stock
An Imprint of Wipf and Stock Publishers
199 W. 8th Ave., Suite 3
Eugene, OR 97401

www.wipfandstock.com

PAPERBACK ISBN: 978-1-7252-8982-6
HARDCOVER ISBN: 978-1-7252-8983-3
EBOOK ISBN: 978-1-7252-8984-0

02/01/21

For Maureen, my big sis, and in memory of Stanley, uncle, big brother, friend.

"I put all my confidence in Him, my sole protection
Is the saving grace that's over me."

BOB DYLAN

Contents

Introduction

WHAT DO YOU THINK of Paul the Apostle?

If you think Jesus is great but aren't too sure of what you think about Paul . . .

If you've read some Paul and find him . . . well, complicated . . .

If you think Paul's teaching is hopelessly out-of-date and needs to be thoroughly revised . . .

If you think that Paul really doesn't like women and wants to put them in their place . . .

If you've grown up with Paul, love Paul and want to understand him better . . .

Then this book's for you!

And if you don't really know him at all and just want to find out—then this might be a good place to start.

I've called it *Paul Distilled*, because we want to boil it all down, see past all the trees to the wood, and get to the heart of what made the man tick. See what is at the core of his thinking. Which might just enable us to go back and take another deeper look at everything he has to say—but that's for you to do when you have finished reading this!

For now, I want us to explore the main driving forces in Paul's thinking, because as we do that, I think you'll find it explosive and inspiring. As we go along, we'll discover he said some seemingly outrageous things in his letters to the various churches to which he wrote, but we'll get to the bottom of these and find out what he was really getting at.

Here was a man of extreme violence, something of a terrorist in his day, utterly opposed to the new groups of Jesus-followers that had sprung up, who ended up becoming one of them, himself tortured and imprisoned, and eventually executed for his views on who Jesus was and what God was doing in the world. For that alone he demands our attention.

And then there are those letters he wrote, some of which we have in our New Testaments, which give us an insight into what he's all about. He never set out to write theology. We shouldn't think of Paul as sitting on the veranda of his villa overlooking the Mediterranean, papyrus at the ready, thinking: "Now how can I explain comprehensively the doctrine of God to these good folks in Philippi? Where do I start?"

It wasn't like that! Paul wrote to these tiny groups of Jesus followers, most of which he'd founded, dotted across the Roman Empire, to address pressing issues that he had heard about, either from them directly or from others. With a pastor's heart, he wanted to help them see what their new-found faith in Jesus the Messiah meant in the situations in whichthey found themselves. He wanted to guide them, help them, and inspire them. Usually he was at pains to point out how much he cared for them and that he was constantly praying for them. Sometimes he cared so much that he got pretty annoyed with them—like the Galatians, for thinking that they might need to add adherence to the Jewish Torah to their faith in Jesus, or the Corinthians, who were listening to preachers who were bad-mouthing Paul.

But here in the practical advice that the letters contain, it's possible to piece together Paul's thinking about God, about Jesus, and about what is happening in the world—his theology. We shouldn't think that that is an easy task, because, of course, we're separated from Paul by nearly two thousand years. He lived in a very different world from ours, with a different language, a different culture . . . a whole different way of thinking.

So we can't expect that everything Paul says to translate directly into our world. We need to be patient and be prepared to learn a bit about Paul's world and the things that influenced him and his thinking. As Christians, we take our Bibles seriously and we want to be able to apply what we find there to our lives—but if we are to do that successfully, we need to tread carefully, always aware of the gap that needs to be bridged between the world of the first century and that of the twenty-first century.

There are two things that heavily influenced Paul's thinking that we need to take account of. First is the fact that Paul was a Jew, a Pharisee, who knew his Jewish scriptures and traditions inside out. We find him, time and time again, quoting from the Old Testament as he presses his arguments in his letters. So paying attention to the Jewish theology that was embedded in Paul's thinking is very important as we try to find out what he thought God had done in Christ.

The other thing is the resurrection of Jesus, the Messiah. The reason Paul's life was turned around so dramatically was that he met the risen Jesus personally. This changed everything for him. Without the resurrection, he realized, there was no value in following Jesus. But from the reality of the resurrection that Paul experienced in that encounter with Jesus on the road to Damascus, everything flowed. We need to keep that firmly in our sights as we read Paul. And it'll be firmly in our sights as *Paul Distilled* unfolds.

I've been studying, wrestling with, Paul for the last thirty years. My PhD thesis focussed on texts in Paul's big letter to the Romans and then I taught Paul for many years in my local university, helping both undergraduates and ministerial students get to grips with Paul's thinking. During the three-month lockdown caused by the health pandemic of 2020, I did a series of ten-minute videos for my church on various aspects of Paul's thought, called *Paul in Ten*, meant to help people understand Paul a bit better and to encourage and inspire them during the difficult days of lockdown. You can find these on YouTube, and they are a kind of companion to this book.

I decided then to convert that material into book form, augmenting some of the material and adding some new stuff. That meant I needed to make the material cohere and fit together properly—and I realized that what I had was a distillation of Paul's thought—what's at the heart of it.

Distillation is a common technique in making perfume. Lots of perfume manufacturers refer to their product as an "essence." An essential oil is what you get through steam or dry distillation. It's the characteristic fragrance of the plant from which it is derived.

Interestingly, although I had taught Paul at a detailed level for many years, trying to distil down his thought to the essence—what's most characteristic of it—sent me scurrying back to his letters and all the major writers on Paul whose works are on my book shelves, and made me think deeply about what it is that made Paul tick.

What I came up with surprised me a little, and I began to realize that at the very heart of things for Paul is simply the love of God. That sparkles everywhere in his writing. And of course, that is demonstrated wonderfully in the death of Jesus. Then there's the resurrection which looms large over every page of his letters and, along with God's love, is right there at the heart of things. The other wonderful re-discovery for me was how central the Holy Spirit is for Paul—God's very presence within and among God's people, and God's power to bring "life to our mortal bodies."

As you read through the book, you'll find other aspects of "essence of Paul"—the new creation, the kingdom of God, justice, peace, care for the poor, lives full of joy and free from anxiety. There's much in Paul that I've left out; and we're only scratching the surface of the subjects we're tackling. I hope you'll go on from here on your own journey of discovery of this man whose thinking and writing has been so influential, not only for Christians, but in the world generally for two thousand years. To help you with that, there are some suggestions for further reading at the end of each chapter.

In addition, I'm hoping that the book might provide a useful starting point for discussion in church home groups, so each chapter has some questions that might be useful in getting started.

Ultimately, my hope is that as you read *Paul Distilled*, you'll get closer to the heart of Paul and it'll help you as you continue to read your New Testament. And I hope, above all, you'll be challenged, encouraged, and inspired with the love of God, the world-changing power of the cross and the resurrection, and the dynamic power of the Holy Spirit.

1

The World Changing Love of God

SUPER-CONQUERORS—REALLY?

As we read Paul's letters, we can't help but be set back on our heels from time to time at some of his statements, which, quite frankly, to our modern ears, sound, well . . . outrageous. Because these are so familiar to many of us, we often read them on automatic pilot and the full force of them doesn't hit us.

Take, for example, his statement toward the end of Romans 8, where he says, "in all these things, we are more than conquerors." The word Paul uses here is a particularly strong one, which we could translate as "super-conquerors." Which really makes it all the more outrageous, when we consider the difficulties of our own lives at times, and for sure, the very real suffering that is going on in our communities and in the wider world.

What on earth are we to make of this statement? Paul sounds like some sort of positive-thinking, self-help guru here with advice that takes no cognizance of the realities of life. It seems like an outrageous thing to say.

HARDSHIP IN ROME

Especially when we consider the situation of the Christians in Rome to whom Paul wrote his letter. They had very difficult lives, much more difficult than most of us. Rome was crowded, people lived in cramped apartments with no sanitation. The night soil was just tipped out the window. If you got sick, there were no doctors or medicine for you—the likelihood was you'd die. Children and mothers died in childbirth and infant mortality was high. Disease could spread rampantly through neighbourhoods. The social distancing we've become used to in the coronavirus pandemic was not an option. Death was an ever-present reality for everybody, and especially for the vast majority of people who lived from day to day, doing their best to survive.

If you have visited poor communities in developing world countries, in slums and rural villages, then that's the sort of situation—and worse—that the first Christians lived in. Rubbish in the streets, vile smells and many people living in tiny rooms. So, in chapter 8 of his great letter to the Jesus-followers in Rome, when Paul says, "I consider that the sufferings of this present time are not worth comparing with the glory about to be revealed to us," he's not talking hypothetically, or about some minor inconveniences. People living in Rome had it tough. Just getting by was sometimes all you could do.

So, when Paul says, a few verses later, "Who will separate us from the love of Christ? Will hardship, or distress, or persecution, or famine, or nakedness, or peril, or sword?" he's not making up a list just to emphasize his point. When we read that, we kind of skim over each of the words Paul uses, because they're not that relevant to us, really.

But when this letter was first read to the Christians in Rome, they recognized every one of these things:

- *hardship*: just being able to get enough money to sustain yourself and your family was a struggle for many of these people.

- *distress*: seeing your children get sick and die. 50 percent of children died before their 10th birthday in the first century.

- *persecution*: following Jesus and not honoring the gods which protected your neighborhood made you a person of suspicion, would make people not want to do business with you, and at times actively oppose you.

- *famine*: hunger was an on-going problem for ordinary people in Rome, many of whom depended on a grain dole by the authorities; Paul himself in 2 Corinthians 11 says he was "often without food."

- *peril*: Rome was a city of great violence—it was a place where slaves were beaten and sexually exploited; where new-born babies were thrown away on rubbish heaps; where political and street mob violence was commonplace; and where the gladiatorial games preserved an atmosphere of violence.

- *the sword*: the sword was regularly used in Rome to enforce its laws and execute people. Actually, capital punishment frequently involved torture, flogging, crucifixion, dismemberment and more.

Paul knew precisely the sort of life-on-the-edge existence of the believers in Rome, and wanted them to know that none of these things, not the hardships of daily life, or even the threat of beatings, torture or execution, could separate them from the love of Christ.

So, don't think for one minute Paul was being trite, or trying to keep his sunny side up, when he told the Jesus-followers in Rome that they are "more than conquerors." He knew the very serious and difficult circumstances they found themselves in.

Actually, they're not that different from the circumstances that Paul found himself in. Paul sought to support his life as a traveling evangelist by making tents and awnings, but an itinerant lifestyle made it difficult to establish a business in each new place and he found it hard to make ends meet. So, he was often "hungry and thirsty, often without food and naked" (2 Corinthians 11:27). On top of that he suffered beatings, imprisonments, and shipwrecks.

So, what does he mean, when, after listing all these hardships that he knew the Romans experienced, he says, "we are super-conquerors"? How can Paul say such a thing to people who were enduring so much? What would it mean to the abused slaves who had become Jesus-followers and part of a Christian community in Rome? Or to the day laborers who couldn't be sure of their income from one day to the next? Or to the migrant workers who were separated from their families? These were all likely members of the little Jesus-following communities in the city.

And how can we, in the challenging circumstances we see all around us, find comfort and inspiration in what Paul has to say?

THE LOVE OF GOD

It all revolves around the subject of the love of God. Love is a major theme in Paul's letters—he mentions love over one hundred times. God, he says, is the God of love and peace (2 Corinthians 13:11); God's love has been poured into our hearts (Romans 5:5); and Christ's love is beyond anything we think we know (Ephesians 3:19). Love was the be all and end all: the greatest thing in the world, for Paul, was love (1 Corinthians 13).

When Paul encountered the risen, living Messiah on the road to Damascus that fateful day, his life was changed. He had been a man so zealous for his ancestral traditions that he was prepared to pursue that zeal with an excess of violence. In fact, he was on his way to continue that onslaught of violence against the first Jesus-followers, when he was stopped dramatically in his tracks. He lost none of his passionate nature and was able to channel that into his new mission to spread the good news of Jesus the Messiah, but the violent, ruthless Paul was changed into a Paul motivated and shaped by his experience of the love of God. The idea that the Son of God loved him and had given himself for him controlled him and urged him on (Galatians 2:20 / 2 Corinthians 5:14). Paul knew above all else, deeply and personally, that God loved him and that nothing could ever separate him from that love.

Now the idea of God's love was one that was part of Paul's heritage as a first century Jew. God, essentially and profoundly, loved his people Israel through all their tortured history, their foolishness and unfaithfulness. Again and again, God had graciously intervened on behalf of his people, and prophets like Hosea, Ezekiel, and Jeremiah talk in quite emotional terms about God's intense love for God's people.

So, this idea of a God who loves, and loves again, and is utterly faithful in that love, despite the unfaithfulness and waywardness and sin of his people and the world, was one that Paul was very familiar with. But, crucially, when Paul encountered the living Christ and he realized how God's love had been most powerfully revealed in Jesus, the sense of that love gripped him and became the driving force in his life. Here's what he said about it:

> Even though I was formerly a blasphemer, a persecutor,
> and a man of violence . . . I received mercy and the grace
> of our Lord overflowed for me with the faith and love
> that are in Christ Jesus (1Timothy 1:13—14).

Paul's scriptures had spoken to him of a God of love and faithfulness, but that love became grounded in a new and ultimate way in the person of Jesus. Jesus was the ultimate expression and embodiment of God's complete and utterly self-giving love.

Christ's death for us is the proof, the demonstration, of God's love, Paul says in Romans 5:8. Christ died for us while we were yet sinners, God's enemies even, when we were completely alienated from God, completely unworthy of such love. And Paul is so taken by this amazing turn of events that he says in Romans 8:32, "He who did not spare his own Son, but gave him up for us all—how will he not also, along with him, graciously give us all things?"

All this must have been utterly remarkable to the people in Rome to whom Paul was writing. This was a city of violence, ruled by the notoriously brutal Nero, where lives were hard and short, and the pagan gods were at best impersonal and capricious, and at worst downright vengeful. If you look at any of the literature from this period, you'll find nothing about the gods loving humanity. People would have found the idea that God loves humanity incredible and even bizarre. So, Paul's insistence on God's love, and of a God who became human and gave his life up for humanity, must have been utterly, utterly astonishing.

The thing about poverty is that it robs you of self-respect. For the slaves and the homeless, and the artisans who were just getting by in the Roman congregations, everything in their lives conspired to tell them they were worthless, that they deserved no better and that things could never be different.

I've seen the same thing first hand, when I visited severely disadvantaged people living in slums in desperate conditions in Indian cities, people who felt they could not even make eye contact with you, so badly did they feel about themselves.

Rome in the first century was very hierarchical—you needed to know your place and you needed to stay there. Honor was an important social value in this world, highly prized by the wealthy elite, who gained it by their military success and their ostentatious wealth. There was little honor left for the great mass of people just trying to get by.

So when Paul told these Roman Jesus-followers that God had shown mercy on them and prepared them for glory (Romans 9:23), it must have sounded incredible. The whole Christian message based on the love and mercy of God was utterly counter-cultural and was, without a doubt, wonderfully good news.

SUPER-CONQUERORS—FOR REAL!

In this amazing passage at the end of Romans 8, Paul goes on to say:

> For I am convinced that neither death, nor life, nor angels, nor rulers, nor things present, nor things to come, nor powers, nor height, nor depth, nor anything else in all creation, will be able to separate us from the love of God in Christ Jesus our Lord.

The little groups of Jesus-followers in Rome needed to know that the love of God is the most powerful thing in the universe. It was greater than anything they would face in the hard circumstances of their lives in Nero's Rome. This, Paul knew, was what would sustain them and give them courage to face the very worst that could assail them. And, of course, the very worst did eventually overtake them.

Just a few short years after Paul had written his letter to them, Nero made the Roman Christians his scapegoats for the deadly fire that left a third of the city a smoking ruin in the summer of 64. Some were torn to pieces by dogs, some were crucified, smeared with pitch and used as nighttime torches. And both Peter and Paul perished around the same time.

The love of God, Paul said, was greater than anything the Romans might face. Ultimately, he said, it's greater than death. In the end, one way or another, some time or another, that's the enemy we all have to face. But not even that could separate the Romans, or can separate us, from God's love.

You and I may not face the hardships that those first Christians in Rome faced. But each of us, like them, need to feel loved. We each need to feel that we are someone who is worth something. Often the way the world treats us, or the way we perceive our achievements, or lack of them, robs us of that.

Our overall psychological well-being—the way we feel about ourselves, the quality of our relationships, and our ability to deal with difficulties—depends on a sense of being valued and loved. Psychological studies indicate that love brings us a sense of security and well-being, and gives us a greater sense of purpose and optimism.

This is backed up by recent neuroscientific studies, which indicate that when we have a sense of being loved, a powerful cocktail of chemicals is released in our brains which reduces fear and makes us feel better.

So Paul knew what he was talking about, when he mentions love all those times in his letters. He knew that an experience of the love of God would enable the Romans—and us—to be super-conquerors in life, no matter what our circumstances may be. The knowledge of God's love, though, was not simply a mental exercise. Paul said it was "poured into our hearts through the Holy Spirit which is given to us." Better felt than telt, as the Scotsman put it. More about the Holy Spirit's role in all this in a later chapter.

When we know that we are loved children of God, it begins to combat the negative self-images we've built up over many years. A sense of God's unconditional love, that God puts inestimable value on our lives, gives us a sense of our intrinsic value, and gives us a framework in which to understand the world and how we fit in. It affects our thinking in powerful ways, giving us the ability to bear life's troubles and difficulties, rather than negative thoughts adding to our woes.

You know, the greatest thing we can ever discover in life is that God loves us. Not just that God loves the world, not just that God loves his people, but that the God of the universe, the creator and sustainer of life—loves me. The one who "spared not his only Son, but gave him up freely," loves me deeply. His love surrounds me, every day. Wherever I am, whatever I am facing, God is for me. "If God is for us, who can be against us?"

And if we know that to be true, then we are super-conquerors. Paul's outrageous statement suddenly becomes not so outrageous. He knew these Roman believers lived in very difficult circumstances; but he knew that God loved them completely. God didn't magically turn their circumstances around; in fact, things eventually got worse for them. But through the risen Christ and his spirit at work within their little communities, God was right there with them, in their hunger and distress, right to the very worst that could come, even if it was death.

I had an uncle, with whom I was very close and who went to be with the Lord a few months ago. My uncle Stanley lived with my family when I was a boy and we remained close friends all our lives. He was a great pray-er, who prayed for me and many others every day of his life. Right up to the end, in all that he suffered from the illness that took him, he knew how completely God loved him and, even in the midst of his intense suffering, he was a super-conqueror. He wouldn't have thought of himself as anyone special, but he knew God loved him and that God was right there with him in the very depth of his suffering. God's love held him as he passed through death into God's presence. "Nothing shall separate us from the love of God."

And God is right here with us too. As I write this, the world is in the midst of a ferocious pandemic which has affected tens of millions and led to more than a million deaths, and is giving rise to widespread economic hardship, domestic abuse, and fear, anxiety, and division. But in the midst of all that, right in the middle of all the problems that this has brought, the reality is that God loves us, Jesus died for us and God is with us. It is possible to be more than conquerors through him who loved us. Because in the end, the worst that we can face is death, the sting of which has been drawn by the victory of Christ's cross and resurrection. And because even now the presence and power of God surrounds us and gives us courage and hope and joy, even in the midst of difficulty and trial.

And that ought to give us confidence, and grace to live, even in the face of the most difficult of circumstances. And, it enables us to be the expression of God's love to a needy world—but more of that our next chapter.

REFLECTION

How does an appreciation of the situation of the Roman Christians to whom Paul wrote affect our understanding of what Paul has to say to them in Romans 8?

What does it mean to say that God loves us?

How important is it to know the reality of God's love in a personal way? What difference does this make to our lives?

What would the word "conqueror" would have meant normally for the Roman believers? How does this contrast with Paul's idea about the word?

Can you begin to contrast the values of the Roman Empire with God's kingdom?

What does it mean for us to be "super-conquerors," in practical terms?

FURTHER READING

Douglas A. Campbell, *Pauline Dogmatics, The Triumph of God's Love*, Eerdmans, 2020, chapter 3.

Patrick Mitchel, *The Message of Love: The Only Thing that Counts*, Inter-Varsity Press, 2019.

2

Love is a Verb

LOVE YOUR NEIGHBOR

WE'VE SEEN THAT GOD's love is right at the heart of Paul's thinking, and how an experience of that love enables us to be, as he puts it, "more than conquerors." But Paul's vision for the love of God goes much further than us being the objects of God's love and having an experience of it. Central to Paul's thought is that Jesus-followers ought to be the expression of God's love to each other and to a needy world. God's love is experienced largely by us through other members of God's family and by the world around by our care, compassion, and action.

Paul, as we've seen, mentions love over one hundred times in his thirteen letters in the New Testament, the sheer number indicating the importance of the theme. Sometimes, as we've seen, he's talking about God's great love for us—which, for Paul, is supremely evidenced in the death of Christ for the undeserving—God "proves his love for us in that while we still were sinners Christ died for us" (Romans 5:8).

This is the foundation for the rest of Paul's many references to love. On just three occasions, Paul mentions our love for God—but the rest of what he has to say is all about us loving others. Now that's interesting, don't you think?

As a Jew, central to his thinking was the teaching of the Torah: Deuteronomy's "You shall love the Lord your God with all your heart, with all your soul, and with all your strength"; and the instruction in Leviticus to love your neighbor as yourself, which is repeated again and again in a variety of ways, including not only the neighbour and family, but the stranger, with a warning against injustice and taking vengeance.

And Paul was also aware of the way that Jesus extended the need to love others beyond neighbors to enemies and that he had said the supreme sign of being his follower was love. In addition, Jesus rolled up the whole of the teaching of Torah into just two commandments, to love God and love your neighbour.

Paul takes this up in Romans 13:9, where he says that all the commandments of the law are summed up in this word, "Love your neighbor as yourself." Love, he goes on to say, is the way in which the whole Jewish law becomes fulfilled.

So, it should be no surprise to us that while Paul only talks a few times about our love for God, he talks again and again about loving others. Because loving others is precisely the way in which we go about showing our love for God. In his letter to the Galatians, where he talks about the importance of faith, Paul says that the only thing that really matters is "faith expressing itself through love." Love is the way in which faith in God works itself out.

If we don't have love, as Paul famously put it in 1 Corinthians 13, we are nothing. All our protestations of love for God, of believing the right doctrines, of our contribution to church meetings, even sometimes, our seemingly good actions—it's all so much excess noise and clamour, if our lives are not characterised by love. Remember too, John's brutally honest: "Those who say "I love God," and hate their brothers or sisters are liars." If we can't love a sister or brother whom we have seen, John says, we cannot love God whom we have not seen (1 John 4:19—20).

And, of course, while Paul specifically mentions love on all these occasions in his letters, that's really just the tip of the iceberg.

We hear him talking again and again about forgiveness, peace, non-violence, kindness, faithfulness, forbearance, and compassion. Love pervades Paul's letters. But it's all summed up by Ephesians 5:2: "Live in love, as Christ loved us and gave himself up for us, a fragrant offering and sacrifice to God." And by 1 Corinthians 14:1 where Paul says simply, "Pursue, seek after, strive for, love."

WHAT IS LOVE?

At this point, we maybe want to ask just what love is. And, of course, a lot of what we think about love we get from popular culture. There's a recently published book entitled *Everything I Need To Know About Love I Learned From Pop Songs.*

Actually, that's maybe not that far from the truth—love is a feeling, something you can fall into or out of, love is sex, or maybe, like the band Foreigner, we just wanna know what love is. Remember the Beatles said "All you need is love"—and then, as Jesus rocker Larry Norman famously observed, they broke up.

And, of course, in our world, the real person to love is yourself. The individual is the centre of the universe. Go check out the number of books on Amazon on self-realization, discovering yourself, being true to yourself. Andy Warhol's prediction in 1968 that everyone would get their fifteen minutes of fame has been fulfilled, except with social media, it might be a few seconds of fame. Selfie culture has overtaken us, with the idea that anyone can become a celebrity, even without skills or talent, depending on your media and marketing know-how. Self-promotion, self-actualization, and self-satisfaction is the name of the game. And our economic systems revolve around the consuming self—because you're worth it, as the L'Oréal advertisement puts it.

We're very far from Paul's idea about love in this sort of territory. But what he said about love was pretty foreign to his original readers too. Their religion and popular philosophy had no conception of the sort of thing Paul was talking about.

LOVE IN PAUL'S WORLD

Let's think for a minute about a couple of people who we might imagine were part of one of the churches to whom Paul wrote. A couple of stories will help (and here I am indebted to Peter Oakes's excellent *Reading Romans in Pompeii*).

Let's think about a couple of people who may have been members of the house churches in Rome to which Paul wrote his letter. First of all, we have Sabina who, along with her husband, had been a slave, but eventually, as was possible in the Roman world of slavery, they managed to buy their freedom. But after that, they struggled to find employment outside the master's household. Eventually they did manage to get some work as stonemasons, just labouring at people's houses or sometimes getting surplus work from workshops.

The labour was really tough, they were getting on in life, and they got paid very little. Getting enough to buy food was a struggle. To be honest, they were nearly destitute.

But one day, a Jesus-follower met Sabina and invited her to a meeting with some of her friends, and there she heard the amazing news about Jesus, a Jewish man who was also God, who loved *her*—an ex-slave and a day labourer—and loved her enough to die for her.

And the people she met started looking out for Sabina and her husband, making sure they had enough to eat, making real their message that God loved her and that Jesus cared for her. Sabina had never encountered anything like this before—in her world people typically thought compassion and mercy were abnormal emotions, character defects to be avoided by anybody rational.

Sabina and her husband became followers of Jesus and found a home in the little group that met in a room in a crowded apartment block.

And then there's Primus, who was a slave in the house of a certain wealthy civic leader in Rome. Primus was a bath stoker—he built the fire for the master's bath: it was a horrible job, dirty, with long hours, and no chance of earning tips and so no chance of ever buying his freedom. Life was brutal for Primus.

But something amazing happened—one of the other slaves who got out of the house a bit running errands for the master told Primus about some people he'd met who were followers of the Jewish God and his son, Jesus, and how they'd been kind, and he'd started going to one of their meetings in a nearby house when he could.

Long story short, Primus went too, and found the amazing sight of householders, slaves, freed people, and homeless people all together, worshipping Jesus.

Nobody was looking down their noses at anybody, as usually happened in Rome. This was a very hierarchical society, where everybody was very conscious of where they were in the pecking order and "associating with the lowly," as Paul put it in Romans 12:16, was not on anyone's radar.

But not only did this diverse group of people meet together, but Primus found that they hugged each other at the end of the meeting—the "holy kiss," they called it, which he thought at first was outrageous and very puzzling.

Primus, with no family, and everything in his life reinforcing a sense of utter worthlessness, found himself amazingly, wonderfully drawn into the circle of love. Suddenly he had a family. For the first time in his life, he had a group of people who loved him and started to look out for him. When Primus heard Paul's letter being read out, he was rocked by the words he heard, "God does not show favoritism." Everyone was equal before God and loved by God; the master of a household was no more a favored member of God's family than his slaves.

More than this, though, Primus would have found Paul's words that he was a "son of God" staggering. In his world, the only person who was the son of God was the emperor himself—this was a claim that successive Caesars had made about themselves for many years. So for a slave like Primus to feel that he had been adopted into God's family must have been mind-bending. And this was not just theory—it was worked out by the practical love and care Primus experienced from his new Jesus-following family.

Primus's and Sabina's stories were like so many in these little groups of Jesus-followers—because they had found a group totally unlike anything else in the empire. There was nothing in the worship of the pagan gods to encourage love and compassion, certainly not towards people who had nothing, and nothing to give you back.

LIVE IN LOVE

When Paul looked at Jesus, he saw what God looked like. He saw what God's love looked like. It loved the unlovely; it loved enemies; it stripped itself of all privilege and humbled itself, coming right in amongst those in desperate need. In his letter to the Philippians, Paul makes this very clear:

> Christ Jesus, who, though he was in the form of God, did not regard equality with God as something to be exploited, but emptied himself, taking the form of a slave, being born in human likeness. And being found in human form, he humbled himself and became obedient to the point of death—even death on a cross.

For Paul, there can no other response possible in the face of the incredible compassion and love of God, than for Jesus-followers to "live in love," and to "pursue" love.

And here really, we have what amounts to another outrageous statement by Paul: "Live in love, as Christ loved us and gave himself up for us." We're charged with loving the world in the same self-sacrificial way that Jesus did. The same self-emptying, humble, serving love that was demonstrated by Jesus in his life and death is precisely what Paul suggests is required of Jesus-followers. Well, that sounds like a very tall order—seriously Paul, is that *really* required?

When Paul looks at the cross, he can find no other response but to reach out in loving action to other brothers and sisters, and to the world, in a way that cares nothing for his own comfort. In fact, as we will see before long, Paul saw the new identity of a Jesus-follower as being Christ-shaped—they were to be "molded to the pattern of Christ" (Romans 8:29). To be a follower of Jesus means a life shaped by the same self-giving love of our Lord. Pretty challenging.

But the love they had for one another and contributing to each other's needs was the thing that sustained these early believers in the very difficult circumstances in which they lived. They "bore one another's burdens" (Galatians 6:2), helping each other in practical ways—in some cases helping each other to survive, making sure everybody had enough to eat, had clothes to wear and somewhere to shelter, and generally supporting each other in the face of the trials that life threw at them in the cities of the Roman empire.

Paul also expected these believers' love for one another to overflow beyond their community to the world around them. He told the Galatians they had to "work for the good of all." And, he was particularly concerned about the poor—as we will explore in more detail later.

He also knew that love extended not only to the Christian community and to their neighbors but to their enemies. This idea of enemy love, which Paul inherited from Jesus, was quite foreign to the Rabbinic teaching that Paul inherited, and there really is no parallel in the Greek philosophical tradition. So, when Paul says in Romans 12, "if your enemies are hungry, feed them" and "bless those who persecute you; bless and do not curse them," this would have been radically different than anything the Romans had encountered. For a vulnerable group of people on the margins and the object of considerable suspicion, with persecution an all-too-real possibility, this was not some hypothetical advice. The dangers facing these Christians was real; enemies were tangible; and reacting in such a way as to bless them, help them, love them was something extraordinary.

And here we are, in our bitterly divided societies, the left not wanting anything to do with the right and vice versa; hate and bile spewing all over social media. How easy it is to get sucked into all of that, such is the power of the media in all its manifestations to incense us and urge us into confrontation. Blessing, not cursing; love those who despitefully use you—that is the way of Jesus. Paul says we are to let the love of Christ control us and urge us on. Live in harmony, love your enemies, says Paul.

We've talked about the inadequate notions of love in popular music. One recent song, though, does get it right. John Mayer's *Love is a Verb*:

> When you show me love
> I don't need your words
> Yeah love ain't a thing
> Love is a verb.
> When you show me love
> I don't need your words
> Yeah love ain't a thing
> Love is a verb.

LOVE IS ACTION

It's not our feelings, it's not words: it's action. An old preacher I heard many years ago said that love is a decision, not an emotion. He said it was a decision for someone else's highest good. That takes the emphasis right away from our own interests, or how we might feel about another person, or our own inclination. As John Mayer says, "you gotta show, show, show, show me . . ."

Because we know that he died for all, Christ's love compels us, Paul says. But even knowing that, it still looks pretty challenging, doesn't it? Let's face it, sometimes loving those in our own Christian community can be pretty tough, never mind loving those we disagree with, or worse still, those who might want to harm us. How is it possible to live such a way, in the imitation of Christ, choosing the best for others consistently?

The good news is that there is a power beyond us, a supernatural power which God gives us to live in this self-denying, world-challenging way. Paul tells us about God's "incomparably great power for us who believe, which is the same as the mighty strength he exerted when he raised Christ from the dead" (Ephesians 1:19—20). Once again, we'll return to discuss this more fully in a later chapter. But it's fantastic, isn't it?—the same power which raised Jesus from the dead is at work within us, enabling us to live in this world-altering, love drenched way.

So, in what way is the love of Christ going to compel us today? How can I live in love? What action will I take today that moves the focus off myself and demonstrates God's love to someone else? It could be as simple as a phone call, or a WhatsApp message to encourage or support someone; it could be the time we spend in prayer for others. But somewhere along the line, it's going to affect our wallets and our time, and it'll cost us something. It might even, as it did for Paul and the first Christians, lead us into danger.

Live in love, as Christ loved us and gave himself up for us.

REFLECTION

How much are we affected by popular notions of love in music, TV, movies and the media? What steps can we take to counteract that?

In what ways can we show love to people we really disagree with and who might be disagreeable?

Is it possible to love "as Christ loved us"?

What practical steps can we take to be more actively loving to: our family; other sisters and brothers in Christ; people we know; those in need?

How important is kindness as a way of showing love? In what ways could I be more kind in my daily life?

FURTHER READING

Douglas A. Campbell, *Pauline Dogmatics; The Triumph of God's Love*, Eerdmans, 2020, chapters 12 & 13.
Patrick Mitchel, *The Message of Love,* Inter-Varsity Press, 2019.
Peter Oakes, *Reading Romans in Pompeii: Paul's Letter at Ground Level*, SPCK, 2009.

3

The Gospel
Firing Our Imaginations

WE'VE THOUGHT ABOUT HOW God's love is at the centre of Paul's thinking and is the motivation and driving force of the life of Jesus-followers. But now we want to put this in the wider context of Paul's thought and to see how it fits in to the bigger picture of what God is doing in the world.

So that brings us to start thinking about the "gospel," which literally means "good news." Paul uses the word from which we get our "gospel" over seventy times in his letters. Which is some indication of how much it was a part of his thinking. In fact, everything in Paul's thinking springs from his understanding of the gospel. So, we want to think about what Paul meant when he talked about the gospel, and to see how that might fire our imaginations and, as a result of that, the way we live.

THE JESUS REVOLUTION

First, though, we need to think for a minute about the good news that Jesus preached.

Mark introduces his gospel as the "beginning of the good news (gospel) of Jesus the Messiah" and immediately references Isaiah in the next verse. A few verses on from the passage Mark quotes in Isaiah 40, it says "Get you up to a high mountain, O Zion, herald of good news . . . say to the cities of Judah, "Behold your God!"" And of course, you remember Isaiah 52: "How beautiful upon the mountains are the feet of the messenger who announces peace, who brings good news, who announces salvation, who says to Zion, "Your God reigns.""

The good news, according to Isaiah, and now according to Mark, and according to Jesus, is that God has arrived on the scene—Behold your God!—Your God reigns! This is the essence of the gospel. God's here; he's bringing his good, peaceful, happy reign to the world—so get on board, get with the programme! Which is why we find the first thing that Mark records Jesus as preaching in chapter one of his gospel is, "The time has come. The rule of God is at hand. Turn around and believe, trust in, give yourselves to, the good news."

The good news, according to Jesus, was that the day of God's reign—the kingdom of God—was arriving. In Jesus's Sermon on the Mount in Matthew's gospel, he tells us about this kingdom—it's a place where the meek, the merciful, the peacemakers, the thirsters after justice thrive and flourish; it's a place where its citizens laugh for joy, even when threatened, where they love their enemies, where they win their battles by prayer, and where they trust God to look after them, no matter what comes their way.

This idea of Jesus bringing the good news about God's reclaiming of his world is consistent throughout all four gospels. God has arrived on the scene; the world is changing; up is down, down is up; follow me and be a part of it—is Jesus's message. And of course, God demonstrated decisively that Jesus had been right by raising him from the dead and beginning the new day of transformation.

PAUL'S GOSPEL OF THE KINGDOM

Which brings us to Paul and his letters to the first groups of Jesus-followers. Paul, as we know, like Jesus, was a Jew, and we might expect his world-view to be pretty similar, forged by Jewish theology and the Old Testament. And, on top of that, Paul actually refers explicitly to the kingdom or the rule of God on fourteen separate occasions in his letters—and actually, if the truth be told, his entire theology is founded on this idea.

Jews of this period expected a day to come when Isaiah's good news of freedom, forgiveness of sins, and a new age of God's peaceful reign on earth would come to pass. There were a variety of views as to how this might come about, but the basic expectation was the same. Although it was anticipated in a variety of ways, people were looking for a Messiah figure, with the common thread the hope for a royal personage who would come and deliver Israel, restore God's people and bring justice to the world. As a Pharisee, this too had been Paul's hope.

The word "Messiah" means anointed one and is all about the coming of God's anointed king. It's a royal title. When the Messiah arrived, so too would God's reign. This would bring justice and peace, and everything would be put to rights. This was good news for Israel and for the world, and it was precisely this good news that "your God reigns" that was at the heart of Paul's gospel.

But, importantly, after his life-changing encounter on the road to Damascus, Paul saw this good news revolving entirely around the advent, death, and resurrection of Jesus. The fact that God had raised Jesus from the dead showed Paul that Jesus was, indeed, the promised Messiah, the King. This was proof, for Paul, that God's new day of salvation, peace and joy had arrived. This, truly, for Paul, was good news.

And we get this spelt out for us in the first few verses of Paul's letter to the Romans. Paul, drawing on his Jewish heritage, talks about the gospel of God, which is the good news, he says, concerning God's Son—here a royal, messianic title—raised from the dead and declared to be Lord, which then requires the obedience of faith.

> Paul, a slave of Jesus Christ, called to be an apostle, set apart for the gospel of God, which he promised beforehand through his prophets in the holy scriptures, the gospel concerning his Son, who was descended from David according to the flesh and was declared to be Son of God with power according to the spirit of holiness by resurrection from the dead, Jesus Christ our Lord, through whom we have received grace and apostleship to bring about the obedience of faith among all the Gentiles for the sake of his name. (Romans 1:1—5)

Many of us have grown up with a version of the gospel that says: I'm a sinner, Jesus died for me, and if I believe in him, then I'll be forgiven and go to heaven when I die. Now none of that is untrue, although it might need some qualification. But for sure it needs to be fitted into the larger picture and focus of what Paul writes about, if it's not to create a false impression of what being a follower of Jesus is all about.

A ROYAL PROCLAMATION

For Paul, the gospel is a royal proclamation about the establishment on the throne of Jesus the Messiah as Lord, which then calls for a response of faith and obedience from all peoples. It's a proclamation of God's rightful ownership of the world. God is reclaiming his world, lost through human rebellion.

The first call is for individuals to respond by faith—clearly a prominent theme in Paul's letters. But it's important to understand what Paul means by the words translated in our New Testaments by "believe" and "faith." In Greek the word for faith carries with it the dual sense of faith and faithfulness, so the sense is more of "believing allegiance." There's no easy believe-ism here. Christian faith is a response of allegiance to the Lord, the Messiah, King Jesus.

But if we were to follow Paul's argument in Romans, the letter in which he most fulsomely explains his understanding of the gospel, we would find in chapter 8 Paul describing the culmination of God's plan of redemption, which involves all of creation—it "waits with eager longing for the revealing of the children of God" and "will itself be set free from its bondage to decay and will obtain the freedom of the glory of the children of God." Tightly coupled to all of this is a glorious future for Jesus-followers who can expect "the redemption of our bodies." This is a clear reference to our resurrection to share in the newly restored creation.

We get another take on Paul's grand vision of the scope of the gospel in Ephesians 1, where Paul makes the colossal claim that because of the resurrection, Christ has been seated "at God's right hand in the heavenly places, far above all rule and authority and power and dominion, and above every name that is named, not only in this age but also in the age to come." This will result in the reconciliation of "all things to himself, whether on earth or in heaven" (Colossians 1:20).

If we were to sum up Paul's gospel, it would be that because of the death and resurrection of Jesus, our God reigns. And that has no end of repercussions.

- Everyone is challenged to align themselves with Jesus and follow him in what will be a costly road of service—what Paul calls the "obedience of faith."

- There is the unleashing into the world, and especially into the lives of Jesus-followers, the presence and power of God in the person of the Holy Spirit.

- Jesus-followers are called to anticipate God's final day of making all things right by working tirelessly for justice and peace here and now—demonstrating the reality of the coming kingdom.

- The governments and rulers of the world, including the tyrants and the despots, have been put on notice that the true ruler of the world is coming in judgement. Their injustice will not be the last word.

- The great enemy of humankind—death—has been defeated and Jesus-followers have the hope of being resurrected to share in the cosmic victory of Christ and the final realization of the kingdom of God.

We'll have more to say about each of these in subsequent chapters.

SOMETHING TO FIRE OUR IMAGINATION

Paul's gospel gives us a big vision, which is truly good news. It includes us as individuals and gives us new life, but it's much, much bigger than that. It's good news for each one of us, but it's also good news for the world. And Paul thought that was something that ought to fire the imagination of the Christians in the churches to which he wrote.

And let's remember, the people in these churches were largely living in poverty; some were in slavery or virtual slavery. They felt their lives could never change—that their lives were fixed by the empire, by fate, by the various spiritual powers that governed the world and by the pull of their own passions, desires and inner demons. So, what did this grand vision of the gospel of the kingship of Jesus, of God reclaiming his world mean for them—and what does it mean for us?

When we turn to Colossians chapters 1 and 2, we read Paul's prayer for the Colossians—he prays for all wisdom and spiritual understanding for them; that they might increase in the knowledge of God; he prays that they would "reach all the riches of full assurance of understanding and the knowledge of God's mystery, which is Christ." To us that maybe sounds very hifalutin, maybe a bit airy-fairy.

But what is Paul praying for here? He's praying that the minds of the Colossians would be expanded, their eyes fully open to the new reality brought by Christ; he puts it another way in Romans 12—when he asks the Romans to be transformed by the renewing of their mind.

He's praying for the Christian imagination to be fired. For the Christians to see past the current state of affairs in the world and in their own lives and to see God at work; to see the mustard seed of the kingdom growing; to see the true state of affairs that the arrogance and blustering of the powers of the world mask. Things are different; things *can* be different. Paul prays for the Colossians' and the Romans' imagination—and ours—to be fired. Can we see the world in the light of the kingship of Jesus?

Paul's proclamation of the reality of the rulership of Christ was a subversion of the dominant version of reality in the first century. Old Testament scholar Walter Brueggemann says that we moderns have become so seduced by the culture around that our creative imagination has become fatally reduced, and that we are numbed, satiated, and sleep-walking our way through life.[1]

Our imaginations are stunted by advertising, the media, people's expectations of us, the way the world is. The only news that we hear is bad news and we're dulled into thinking that the way things are, is the way that things will ever be. As Bob Dylan put it in an interview recently, "All we see is good-for-nothing news . . . It stirs people up. Gossip and dirty laundry. Dark news that depresses and horrifies you."

We're being continually shaped and molded by the world around us. But the good news about the reign of King Jesus that Paul preached is that it can liberate our thinking and imaginations, if we let it.

We need to let Paul's gospel and his vision of the transformative power of Christ permeate our thinking and imaginations. We need to let the alternative reality of the New Testament, that of the good news of the arriving kingdom of God, wake us up from the numbness that is induced by everyday life. We need to start envisaging a new reality for ourselves, for our community together and for our world.

Here's the ultimate reality: God has raised Jesus from the dead. Jesus is risen, and the world has changed. God's new age has burst in.

1. Brueggemann, *Interpretation and Obedience*, 185.

But we look around and, like Bob Dylan says in his song, everything is broken. For Paul's tiny communities meeting together in the cities of the Roman Empire, in one sense nothing had changed. Church members were still slaves; some of them were persecuted for their faith; life was still a challenge.

LIVING THE GOSPEL

But they began to live in a new way. They started to love one another in a revolutionary way. They supported one another through the hardship. They started caring for their neighbours. Before long they were getting a name for the way they loved each other and their communities. They were beacons of light in a dark place. They imagined their world could be different, and they began to live as if it were. And within a couple of centuries their faith had spread all over the world.

Within fifty years of Paul writing his letter to the Romans, it's reckoned that the number of Christians in the city had increased by at least seven-fold—and this despite Nero's executions in the 60s. By the year 350AD, there were likely over thirty million Christians in the Roman Empire. Much of this was down to the way in which these early believers modelled a transformative way of life, showing the world around the reality of the kingdom of God. Tertullian, the second century Christian leader and author in North Africa, said, "It is our care of the helpless, our practice of loving kindness that brands us . . . "Only look," they say, "look how they love one another!""

Unlike any other groups in the empire, every week, generation after generation, Christians collected money for widows, orphans, the sick, and those in prisons. Before long, well-organized networks of social security had developed, showing the world that there was a new way of being human that was based on love.

Can we imagine a world transformed by the love of God? Experiencing the peace of God? Can we imagine our own lives and church communities breaking out of the old mold of the world's self-centredness, greed, and inequality? Of course, we know that the wholesale transformation of the world awaits that final day of God's renewing of the cosmos. But can we imagine some of that into the present?

When you read the first three chapters of Ephesians and Philippians 3 and Romans 8, you realize that Paul's vision is for Jesus-followers to be signs of the day of resurrection right here and now. So that's the challenge for us: can we break free from the mind-imprisoning culture of the world around to imagine a different future for ourselves, our families, our churches, and our world?

The gospel is that because of the death and resurrection of Jesus, our God reigns. Dare we believe that and let that fire our imaginations about a new way of being human?

We are called to be part of a revolution. As we've already seen, it's a revolution of love. It can start with small acts of kindness, of compassion, of reaching out to others in need. But never underestimate the power of love; it can change us. It can change the world.

REFLECTION

What implication does understanding the gospel as a royal proclamation have for our lives? For our Christian community?

How ought we to "anticipate God's final day of making all things right"?

The gospel message affects both individuals and the world. Have Christians got the right balance of understanding of this?

In what ways could we imagine our world to be different? Our family, our church, our local community?

What steps could we take to make what we imagine a reality and a witness to the transformational power of the gospel?

FURTHER READING

Scot McKnight, *The King Jesus Gospel*, Zondervan, 2011.
Rodney Stark, *The Rise of Christianity*, HarperOne, 1997.
Tom Wright, *What Saint Paul Really Said*, Lion Books, 1997.

4

The Cross-Shaped God

THE CROSS IS CENTRAL

ABSOLUTELY CRUCIAL TO PAUL'S understanding of God's love and the good news was the death and resurrection of Christ. The cross, in other words, the death of Christ, Paul said was "the power of God to us who are being saved," and it was the means by which God had brought peace—shalom—to the world and reconciled humans to God. Sometimes Paul uses the phase the blood of Christ, again signifying his death, which brings humankind "near" to God.

It's also the supreme demonstration of the incredible love of God for humankind.

Paul's letters are shot through with references to the death of Christ and he explains its meaning and effects in a variety of ways to bring out the cataclysmic impact of this event. Christ's death, he says is "for us," and he uses words like redemption, forgiveness, adoption, reconciliation, and sacrifice for sin to help plumb the depths of its meaning. He even can refer to the cross as a "triumph," comparing Christ's victory over the power of evil to the victory parade of the returning Roman general.

With the wealth of ways which Paul gives us to think about the meaning of Christ's death, it's best not to get too hung up on any one of them as the most important. Each helps us to understand a different aspect of what Jesus has done for us and for the world. Despite theologians' best attempts to fully explain how exactly Christ's death deals with sin and brings humanity into relationship with God, from a position of what Paul calls in unforgiving terms as "estranged" and even "God's enemies," the New Testament is really much more interested in the results of the cross in individuals and the world.

What's more, it's important to realize that Christ's death does not stand on its own—it only makes sense along with the resurrection. A friend of mine tells the story of a church home group here in Northern Ireland, many years ago, when Protestants and Catholics who have been terribly divided for a long time were taking small steps to reconcile, and two nuns attended a church group meeting in someone's home. Some of those from a Protestant background in the group were still quite stuck in their prejudices and their preconceived ideas of what they thought Catholics believed.

So one evening, the two sisters were late for a meeting, when the group was discussing the meaning of the death of Christ. After they arrived someone decided to ask them if they believed that it was the death of Christ alone that secured salvation. The two sisters replied straightaway that no, they were sure that more than the death of Christ was needed for salvation. Aha, gotcha, thought the questioner, his prejudices confirmed. Only to be deflated by the next part of the response: "not just Christ's death, but his resurrection also." Touché!

But there are important things to be gained from thinking about Christ's death on the cross.

First of all, along with the resurrection, it is the way in which God has dealt with sin. That's not a word that many people are comfortable with these days, but whatever you want to call it, there is terrible evil in the world, and always has been. War, slavery, torture, abuse of women, ethnic cleansing, discrimination, racism—the list goes on. And that's even before we get to wrong-doing on a personal level. There is a big problem.

And when we read Paul, he's not at all optimistic about the human condition. Even when we want to do the right thing, we end up frustrated, he says in Romans 7. Paul calls this condition of human powerlessness the "flesh." The end result is death, God's judgement on evil.

Paul's sense is that the death of Christ is "for our sins." Where Christ takes on our nature of flesh and submits himself to the evil and violence of humanity, so that the flesh is executed on the cross, with God raising Christ to a new, liberated life. In Romans 8, Paul says that what the Torah (or anything else for that matter) could not do, "God did, by sending his own son in the exact form of sinful flesh to atone for sin."

The cross and the resurrection were God's way of dealing with both sin and death, making an entirely new creation possible. Paul goes on to explain that Jesus-followers are "in Christ," and so participate in Christ's death and resurrection, making possible a completely new way of life, starting right now. More of that in subsequent chapters.

ADOPTION

An important result of the cross and resurrection that is very relevant in today's world is what Paul terms adoption. In Romans 8, after telling the Romans that, because of what Christ has done, they are no longer "in the flesh," he goes on to tell them that they are now counted as children of God; they've been adopted into God's family. This was a very powerful metaphor in Paul's world and Paul really deepens our understanding of what God has done for us in Christ by using it.

The basic unit in Roman society in the 1st century was the household, which was effectively ruled by the father—it was a patriarchal, androcentric society. People didn't think of themselves so much as individuals as part of a household—and a household typically involved children, slaves and dependent business suppliers.

Bringing someone into the household through adoption played an important part in this world. Emperors would adopt men with the sole intention of having a successor, and adoption was often used to maintain a family name or property. When adoption took place in the Roman world, through a complicated legal procedure, adopted sons became no less important than biologically born offspring—they took on the same legal status as real sons. They laid aside their old name and acquired the name of the new family—fundamentally they transferred from one family to another, with all the attending privileges and responsibilities. In effect, for the adoptee, a new life started.

All this, of course, the Roman Jesus-followers were familiar with. So when Paul talks about adoption in chapter 8 of his letter to them, he was showing, by means of a social practice they know well, just what happens because of what Christ had done for them. In the Roman family, the head of the household took the initiative and brought someone into his household to share in the legal status, the protection, the economic well-being, of that group. Salvation, says Paul, is just like this: it's God taking an outsider—one who does not belong—and bringing them into a new family, right into the heart of God's family.

And if we are now fully God's children as a result of this transfer, then, says Paul, in 8:17, we are heirs—heirs of God and co-heirs with Christ. Now, interestingly, in Roman law, the heir was understood to be the embodiment of the father—the father lived on, so to speak, in the son—and, more interestingly, not from the time of the father's death, but from the time of the son's adoption.

All of which makes Paul's adoption metaphor a very rich one indeed for us. We have been transferred from our old family into God's family. We are not just in by the skin of our teeth—we've got full legal status, we're completely part of the family, we're fully heirs of all that God has for us in this life and in the kingdom to come—and, we embody the head of the household, God himself. Wherever we go, we are to represent God, we are to bring his presence into whatever situation we find ourselves in. That's what it means to be part of God's family.

Paul is writing to a very mixed group of people, many of whom had every reason for a lack of self-esteem. Some of the people in the church were at the very bottom of the pile—they were slaves, just somebody else's property to be ordered around, beaten or sexually abused at will; some were homeless, doing whatever work anybody might give them to scratch a living; some were Jews, who suffered anti-semitism in Rome and a lack of recognition of the Jewish background of the faith even in the Christian church. For each of these people, Paul's talk of adoption was very good news—God had accepted them, brought them into the inner circle, loved them and made them his representatives. For the recipients of Paul's letter, this was counter-cultural, this was fantastic.

But it's not so different in our world, either, is it? Poverty, hunger and war afflicts a huge proportion of the world's population. The vulnerable—children, women, and the old—are usually the victims. Everything says to these people—you're worthless, you don't count, you're nothing. For those of you who have been in developing world situations, you'll know that, very often, when you meet desperately poor people, they will not even look you in the eye. That's what poverty does to a person—it robs them of their dignity, their self-esteem.

In such situations, the gospel really is good news to the poor, where people are brought into a loving family where their needs are met, where people show by their actions that they count, that they mean something. When the gospel is lived out and demonstrated, oppressed people can begin to lift their heads again with the sense that they matter, because they're part of God's family.

But alienation and despair and lack of self-esteem is not just the lot of the developing world—we see it all around us in the world that we inhabit, on our own streets. Ten per cent of 16 to 24-year-olds say they feel lonely, lack companionship, or feel left out or isolated, and this is particularly marked in richer countries. More people than ever before are living alone around the world. In a world where 40 percent of Americans say they feel lonely or isolated, where nearly half of Britons over 65 consider the television or a pet their main source of company, and where, in Japan, there are more than half a million people under 40 who haven't left their house or interacted with anyone for at least six months, the message of adoption into God's and the Christian family has got to be good news.

The message here is that there is a loving God who values us as individuals, who loves us, and who welcomes outsiders into his family. This is a message we all need to hear and let fill us. When life slaps us down, when disappointment hits, when we just aren't making it, we need to know, deep in our hearts, that we're part of God's family. He hasn't just opened the door and let us into the hallway—God has carried us right into the kitchen to be in the heart of family life with everybody else. God loves us, we're his children, we belong. No matter what lies the world tells us about ourselves at times, each of us is valuable to God, we're in his family, we can hold our heads up.

THE CROSS-SHAPED GOD

The extent of God's love for us is shown by the incredible action God took to make us his children. And that action is cross-shaped. In fact, for Paul, we must think of God himself as cross-shaped. An important passage to understand Paul's thinking about God and the meaning of the cross is Philippians 2:5—11.

> Let the same mind be in you that was in Christ Jesus, who, though he was in the form of God, did not regard equality with God as something to be exploited, but emptied himself, taking the form of a slave, being born in human likeness. And being found in human form, he humbled himself and became obedient to the point of death—even death on a cross. Therefore God also highly exalted him and gave him the name that is above every name, so that at the name of Jesus every knee should bend, in heaven and on earth and under the earth, and every tongue should confess that Jesus Christ is Lord, to the glory of God the Father.

Paul here makes a radical claim about the identity of God. Paul told the Corinthians that he preached a "crucified Christ," indicating the enduring cross-shaped identity of the Messiah. But here he indicates that the cross in fact reveals the very nature of God's being.

Most of our translations say, "although he was in the form of God," but New Testament scholar Michael Gorman suggests there is a good argument for translating this as *"because* he was in the form of God."[1] Which would then indicate that Christ emptied and humbled himself precisely *because* he was in the form of God. In other words, it is in God's very nature to give himself in such a way. Christ's self-humbling in his incarnation and death reveals the very essence of God—utter, self-giving love.

In any case, the entire passage, when we understand Christ's identity as part of the Godhead—in the form of God—is quite clear about the incredible self-giving of God. There is an emptying, a self-humbling, a self-giving, that beggars belief. And not simply that the Messiah would "be found in human form," but that he would be prepared to be executed on a cross.

The cross clearly refers to the Roman means of execution, crucifixion, which was an utterly brutal means of killing someone, designed to cause maximum pain for a prolonged period, resulting in a slow and agonizing death. It was meant to utterly humiliate the victim, who was stripped naked and left to hang for days in shame. Romans typically crucified slaves, those considered terrorists, and disgraced members of the military. It declared loudly the ruthlessness of imperial power, sending a clear message to everyone about the frightening violence of the state. It was so brutal and disgraceful that it wouldn't have been spoken of in polite company.

Paul talks about the "offense" of the cross—it was the epitome of utter shame and degradation to pagans and a sign of "cursing" for Jews, according to the Torah. In the first chapter of his letter to the Corinthians, he says that the cross looks like "foolishness" to their neighbors. The Christian message of a crucified God must have looked utterly crazy in this world. It was shocking and

1. Gorman, *Participating in Christ*, 36–39.

repulsive—gods upheld the world and inflicted punishment, they didn't suffer it themselves. "You're telling me your god became a weak, powerless man and let others torture him and then crucify him? What nonsense!"

But here is the mind-bending reality of what God is like. Weakness becomes strength. Non-violence overcomes violence. Love conquers all. The prophet Isaiah is right—truly God's ways are not our ways.

The cross is the end point of the self-emptying of God—not simply the taking on of humanity but being executed like a criminal in the most shameful, brutal way possible in the first century. So here we have the stark expression of who God is—the cross shows God's nature to be utter love, naked, selfless self-giving. This is the supreme demonstration, Paul says explicitly in Romans 5, of God's love for us.

THE CROSS-SHAPED LIFE

If God and the Messiah can be said to be cross-shaped, then so too are Jesus-followers. Jesus said that his followers had to "take up their cross and follow him"—a statement that must have sounded both bizarre and appalling to his hearers, but it is clear that from the beginning Christians expected to have to follow the difficult path that Jesus had trod.

Paul tells both the Galatians and the Romans that Jesus-followers have been "crucified with Christ." In Romans 6, he explains that in baptism, believers have been baptized into Christ's death. Given the offensiveness of crucifixion for the members of these first century communities, what did Paul mean by this? And what might this mean for us too, who have become so used to the symbol of the cross, that it has been largely stripped of its awfulness by familiarity and time?

New Testament scholar, Tom Wright, says that Jesus-followers are called to "cruciform authenticity," by which he means to be true to the cross-shaped love and action of God. Michael Gorman describes this as "participating in and embodying the cross."[2] He suggests, however, that we ought not to focus on the cross per se but on the crucified—the living Jesus, the crucified Messiah, who indwells individuals and communities, and so enables them to live in the self-sacrificing way that he did.

For many Jesus-followers, from those in Paul's day right through to Christians in today's world, whose lives are blighted by persecution and despotic regimes, this has meant real suffering for their faith, even to the point of death. Most of us will not have to face this, but the call to the cross-shaped life has not gone away.

There are opportunities everywhere we look to deny ourselves. To turn away from the normal way of things—from the self-pleasing, the consuming, the constant entertainment seeking, the easy, the pleasure hunting, all the stuff that is just normal in our world. And instead to find ways to serve others, to put others first, putting our hands into our wallets, and grabbing time out of our schedules and leisure periods to demonstrate to the world the reality of the crucified and risen Messiah.

The cross shows the incredible love of God, the extreme lengths to which God has gone to be able to welcome us into his family. It shows where real power in the universe lies—not in power-grabbing and violence, but in love. And it points the way for us to live truly human lives—in ways that are cross-shaped, where love is the essence of our existence.

REFLECTION

What is sin? Why is it difficult to talk about these days?

What does it mean to say that Christ died "for us"?

How does thinking about God as "cross-shaped" help our understanding of God?

What would a cross-shaped life mean for us?

---

2. Gorman, *Participating in Christ*, 33, who also quotes Tom Wright.

What does Paul's talk of our adoption into God's family mean for each of us?

FURTHER READING

Michael Gorman, *The Death of the Messiah and the Birth of the New Covenant*, Cascade, 2014.

Bruce Longenecker, "What did Paul think was wrong in God's world?" in Bruce Longenecker (ed.), *The New Cambridge Companion to St. Paul*, CUP, 2020.

5

The Resurrection has Begun

THE STANDING UP OF DEAD CORPSES

THE GOOD NEWS—THE GOSPEL—IS all about God coming to re-claim his world and about the incredible love of God which has its ultimate realization in the death of Christ "for us." But Paul shows clearly that the resurrection of Jesus is right at the heart of things. The cross would mean nothing if it weren't for the resurrection. Without it, Paul says, our faith is "in vain."

We've thought already about some outrageous things Paul said. And when we come to the subject of resurrection, just about *everything* he has to say is outrageous. Because, let's be clear: when Paul and the other New Testament writers talk about resurrection, they mean bodily resurrection. The phrase Paul uses, "resurrection from the dead" literally means the "standing up of dead corpses."

In the space of a few short months, I've suffered the loss of an uncle, two cousins, a brother-in-law, and two good friends. For those of you, who like me, have experienced bereavement, you know that dead is dead. Life has come to an end, and we talk about the remains, which we put into the grave. With all our medical technology and advances, we can never do anything about the fact of death.

So, talk about resurrection, bodies being raised to life again, is just very hard to get our minds around. It is, quite simply, outrageous. But for Paul, resurrection is right at the very heart of things. Take it away and you've no Christian faith left. We can say that Jesus was a good person, his teaching is important, the golden rule is great—but simply to say all that is rather to miss the point, which Paul makes quite forcibly in 1 Corinthians chapter 15.

> If Christ has not been raised, your faith is futile and you are still in your sins. Then those also who have died in Christ have perished. If for this life only we have hoped in Christ, we are of all people most to be pitied . . . If the dead are not raised, "Let us eat and drink, for tomorrow we die."

Paul's logic is inescapable: if Jesus has *not* been raised from the dead, then there is no such thing as resurrection for the rest of us. Death is the end, and we might as well make the most of the short time we have on this earth.

So what made Paul so sure about Jesus's resurrection? Paul knew just as well as we do that dead is dead. Death was all around Paul and the people of the Mediterranean world of the first century—we've mentioned already the low life expectancy of people in this world, and the dangers of becoming ill. Add to that the danger of fire sweeping through your neighborhood and the violence in the streets, and you have a situation where everyone was aware of someone dying on a regular basis.

This was Paul's world, so he wasn't some fanciful, wishful thinker. And remember, he didn't start out believing all this resurrection stuff that he started hearing about Jesus when he was a young, zealous Pharisee. In fact, he was so dead set against it that he launched a violent assault against followers of Jesus, so convinced was he of the dangerous nature of their assertions.

But here, in 1 Corinthians 15, he gives us what is the very earliest account of people having encountered the risen Jesus, including Peter, the twelve apostles and, of course, himself. Interestingly,

Paul also mentions an appearance to "more than five hundred brothers and sisters at one time, most of whom are still alive." In other words, a sizeable group of people, themselves still alive, to whom his readers could go and check.

For Paul, the resurrection was crucial. Because if Jesus is raised, he *is* the Messiah, and if so, he is the world's true Lord. If Jesus is raised, then God's new creation has begun. This meant at least a couple things to Paul, both of which should make us very excited.

First, as a Pharisee, Paul expected a general resurrection for God's people at the end of time. But God raising Jesus from the dead with a new, transformed body meant that the general resurrection had begun. It had been brought forward in time. Jesus was the first of a long line of people who would follow.

Paul saw those who believed in—adhered to, gave allegiance to Jesus—as being "in Christ." This meant that they would be resurrected too, with new transformed bodies. Our resurrection will be like Jesus's resurrection—Paul says "Christ has been raised from the dead, the first fruits of those who have died."

Hence Paul saying in 1 Corinthians 15 that our resurrection bodies will be imperishable, glorious, powerful, and spiritual. Note when Paul says "spiritual," it doesn't mean ethereal, ghostly. It's a spiritual *body*. The sense here is a body animated by the spirit of God. It's a physical body but transformed. Remember the gospel accounts of the resurrected Jesus?—recognized by his disciples, able to be touched, and yet able to merge through doors and walls. Jesus-followers, who are "in" the Messiah, then, will be resurrected, just as he was, and with recognizable, but transformed bodies, like his. The Lord Jesus Christ, Paul says, "will transform our lowly bodies so that they will be like his glorious body" (Philippians 3:21).

Heaven, you see, in Paul's thinking was not a celestial city in the sky to which we float after death. Heaven was God's realm, God's space, which Paul expected to come to transform the earth. Remember Romans 8 where Paul says that creation itself will be set free from its bondage to decay, which of course tallies with

Revelation's picture of a new heaven and a new earth, where God will dwell with his people. Paul looked forward to a day when sin and evil would be utterly defeated.

All this leads Paul to these glorious words of Christian hope at the end of 1 Corinthians 15:

> When this perishable body puts on imperishability, and this mortal body puts on immortality, then the saying that is written will be fulfilled: "Death has been swallowed up in victory." "Where, O death, is your victory? Where, O death, is your sting?"

For the Corinthian believers who saw death all around them, these were tremendously comforting words. And for us too, who have lost loved ones, and maybe some of us who are facing that final enemy right now—and for all of us who will face it sooner or later. Jesus is risen. Death has been swallowed up in victory. As sure as Jesus has been raised from the dead, so will we be as well!

THE RESURRECTION HAS BEGUN

But there's another important aspect to the resurrection of Christ for Paul. Everything has changed with the resurrection of Jesus. God's new age has broken into this present age. The life of the age to come, the very life of heaven, has broken into the world. God's new creation has begun. Paul says in 2 Corinthians 5: "So, if anyone is in Christ, there is a new creation: the old order has passed away; see, everything has become new!"

Paul for sure looks forward to the resurrection that began with Jesus, that we all will experience, and the renewing of the cosmos. But that day has *already* started to break into the world, and God has called us to work with him—to be his co-workers in Paul's language—to *anticipate* the final resurrection in our life here and now. Jesus, as Tom Wright puts it, is "God's-future-arrived-in-the-present";[1] a new way of being human has been opened up and

---

1. Wright, *Surprised by Hope*, 57.

we who belong to Jesus are charged with transforming the present, empowered by his Spirit.

There's a sense, actually, in which we already participate in the resurrection. In Romans 6, Paul says that in baptism we were effectively buried with Christ. Our old self, our previous way of life, was "crucified with Christ" and we were united with him in death. The other half of the baptism story is that we are now "alive to God in Christ Jesus." We've begun already to share in Christ's resurrection. There is, as Paul puts it, "a new creation."

Our resurrection has begun! Paul expresses this by his phrase "in Christ," which occurs more than seventy times in his letters. As a result of this, as Paul tells the Corinthians, we have the "mind of Christ"—a resurrected mind if you will. Which means that life can be, and is, gloriously different.

A while ago when I was on holiday in the South of France, I visited the little medieval town of St Paul de Vence, and was delighted to get a tee-shirt printed with a shoal of fish, all headed in the same direction, with one lone red-colored fish swimming against all the rest. Underneath were the words: "Think different, people of St Paul."

Because in Christ our old selves have been crucified and we've now begun to share in Christ's resurrection, we are free to "think different." There are new possibilities to be free from destructive practices and habits, and from the obsession with our own comfort, convenience, and pleasure.

When you read Romans chapter 6, you get a sense of the newness of life that Jesus-followers experience. Paul seems almost dangerously incautious in his talk about "being freed from sin," and sin not having "dominion over you." Paul is not naïve—he was only too aware of the dreadful behaviour of some people in the church in Corinth—but he was very clear about the fact that something real and significant had happened to Jesus-followers, and that they could experience a life free from the dominating power of sin if they presented themselves "to God as those who have been brought from death to life."

There's an amazing musician who played in the New York area in the 1950s and 60s, called Reverend Gary Davis. He was blind but was a jaw-droppingly good guitarist. He sang mostly gospel blues and one of his songs was *Great Change Since I Been Born*. The singer's got a new song, he walks a new road and "things I used to do, I don't do no more." The song captures the turn around and change that becomes possible "in Christ." We dare not underestimate this; we ought to expect God's resurrection life to free us, energize us. and empower us.

BEING THE RESURRECTION

But not only did Paul see these little communities of newly alive-to-God people that he'd founded as experiencing the resurrection life of Jesus in their own lives and being, he thought that individually and together they should be a demonstration to the world of God's new resurrection world. He said that they shone like stars in the world; he said they were God's handiwork, or works of art. They were to be demonstrations of the resurrection life of God in the midst of a violent, unjust, and unhappy world.

For Paul, something dramatic has happened in the world. Jesus-followers have been rescued from the power of darkness and transferred into a new kingdom, a new way of being, the kingdom of God's beloved Son (Colossians 1:13). He won't let us underestimate the incredible new reality in which we now live.

All this because of the resurrection of Christ. Paul says in Romans 8: "If the Spirit of him who raised Jesus from the dead dwells in you, he who raised Christ from the dead will give life to your mortal bodies also through his Spirit that dwells in you." That resurrection life will be ours after we die, but it begins right now. Christ's resurrection life is ours now: the old has passed away, the new has come.

What might all this mean for us? Well, we've thought already about the loving nature of God's kingdom and the fact that we are called to "walk in love." That has far-reaching implications for our individual lives. God's love and power has broken into our lives and set us free from the self-doubt, self-centredness, and self-absorption that is so destructive for ourselves and for others to whom we're connected. The resurrected new creation, the new in-Christ reality enables us to be able to love in an entirely new way that sets us free and those around us. Because of the resurrection, Paul's tall order that we "live in love, as Christ loved us" is really possible. There's the small matter of the Holy Spirit as well, of course! But we'll get to that before long.

RESURRECTION LIFE: JUSTICE, PEACE AND JOY

In Romans 14 Paul tells us that this new era of resurrection, this new realm, or kingdom, to which we've been transferred consists of justice, peace, and joy in the Holy Spirit. Those are to be the characteristics of resurrected lives and communities.

Instead of justice, some of our bibles read righteousness. But there's good reason to translate the word Paul uses as justice. Which at the heart of things is what our world needs desperately. For things to be put right, made equitable and fair.

We all know the terrible injustices that go on everywhere in the world, including our own nation. The health crisis we've been experiencing affects poor communities around the world disproportionately and really shows up the inequities and injustices that exist. The problem of racism has been exposed as endemic in the United States and Europe, and there's a long way to go to address the systemic inequalities.

And that's just the tip of the iceberg, as we look around at the way those who are poor and powerless are exploited by powerful vested interests. Things aren't right and need to be put right. Christians are to be those who, by the just, fair, and compassionate way they live, expose injustice and show there is a better way to live.

God's new transformed world will be a world of peace, where the wild wolves and leopards and lions lie peaceably with lambs and kids. So, peace is to be the hallmark of Christian communities, where people live at peace with one another, and pursue peace with their neighbors. This is utterly counter-cultural in a world where division and conflict, whether it's at the level of social media or relations between nations, are the norm. Christ's kingdom is fundamentally a peaceful one and we are called to demonstrate that by our peacefulness and our peace-making.

And joy in the Holy Spirit: the hallmark of God's new era always, always is joy. With Christ's resurrection, there is a new reality that has broken into the world and into our lives, a foretaste of what God's new world will be like on Christ's return. That's a reason for rejoicing, despite the current brokenness of the world. We get an incredible view of how this can play out in Paul's letter to the Philippians. Paul, himself in prison in dreadful conditions and unsure whether he will be executed or not, tells the Philippians, who are in some considerable difficulty because of opposition from their neighbors, to "rejoice, again I say rejoice!" It's because the "Lord is near"—probably with the dual sense of being at hand and coming back. The resurrection of Jesus and all it means gives Jesus-followers a deep-seated joy which is independent of our circumstances.

The world is waiting to see the resurrection joy in our lives, joy that overflows into lifestyles of justice and peace. In the midst of all that's wrong in the world, we are to demonstrate the justice and peace of God's kingdom. It's time to let Christ's resurrection life flourish in our own lives and spill out in our commitment to justice and a generous way of life.

The Lord is risen! He is risen indeed.

REFLECTION

Has there been more emphasis on Jesus's death than on his resurrection in your experience of church? If so, what has been the result of that?

What is the importance of seeing "heaven" as a renewed cosmos rather than a golden city in the sky?

How does the idea of our resurrection affect our lives here and now?

Have we underestimated the reality of being "in Christ" and the transformation that brings? How can an understanding of this affect our lives?

What does "resurrection life" in our Christian community look like to the world around? What ways can we, individually and as a group, be demonstrations of resurrection justice, peace, and joy?

FURTHER READING

J. R. Daniel Kirk, *Unlocking Romans: Resurrection and the Justification of God,* Eerdmans, 2008.

N. T. Wright, *The Resurrection of the Son of God*, SPCK, 2003.

Tom Wright, *Surprised by Hope*, SPCK, 2008.

6

The Life-Giving Spirit

PEOPLE OF THE SPIRIT

IF THERE'S ONE THING that's clear about the little groups of Jesus-followers dotted around the Mediterranean in the first century AD, it's that they were communities of the Spirit. These were extraordinary groups of diverse people who loved each other, cared for each other, were full of joy, despite the difficulty of their lives; and when they met together, they prayed, they prophesied, they spoke in tongues, they sang, they saw God moving amongst them in power, with miraculous things happening at times. When they met together, things got lively!

Yes, they had their problems and sometimes things got a bit out of control, as we know from Paul's letters to the Corinthians—and, to be clear, Paul did not attribute that to the action of the Spirit. But they had a very real sense of the presence and power of God amongst them because of the Holy Spirit. The Spirit filled them, gave them hope, gave them understanding, gave them gifts to encourage and serve one another, and filled them with joy enabling them to live out their new resurrection life.

And what of Paul himself? Well, he told the Corinthians that he spoke in tongues more than them all, he prayed for the sick and saw miraculous things happen. He told the Romans that his proclamation of the good news of Christ was attested, "by the power of signs and wonders, by the power of the Spirit of God," and the Corinthians that he didn't rely on fancy talk, but on a "demonstration of the Spirit and of power."

Paul speaks of being taken up to heaven in the Spirit where he heard and saw things he could not talk about. He talks about an extraordinary sense of joy in the midst of suffering in his letter to the Philippians. This is the man that we think of as a great scholar of his Jewish scriptures, a theologian, a thinker. But that should not blind us to the fact that Paul was a man of the Spirit.

The Holy Spirit was the air that Paul and his congregations breathed. The Spirit pervaded their meetings. The Spirit filled their communities and individual Christians. What was going on?

THE SPIRIT FUELS GOD'S NEW FUTURE

We've already talked about how Paul saw everything as having changed because of the coming of Christ. This was because of two things: the resurrection of Christ and the subsequent gift of the Spirit. God's future had broken into the present and everything had begun to change.

The word for Spirit occurs over a hundred and forty times in Paul's letters, the vast majority of these referring to the Holy Spirit. That's an indication of how important this is.

For Paul, the resurrection of Christ was the beginning of the End, the turning of the ages. The final event was yet to come, but the future had now broken into the present. And that future was brought by, and enabled by, the Holy Spirit, the very presence and power of God amongst God's people. Paul's Jewish tradition taught him that the Spirit was to be the sign that God's future had arrived. It was the sign that the messianic age had arrived—it was the sure evidence that that future had begun and a guarantee that it would eventually become a full reality.

As we await Christ's coming to renew the cosmos, we even now live the life of the future by the power of the Spirit. The full and final realization of God's future is so certain because of the resurrection that Jesus-followers live a radically new life, made possible by the life-giving Spirit of God.

Paul refers on three occasions to the Spirit as a "down payment"—regularly used in Paul's world, as in ours. as the first instalment of the total amount due. Ephesians 1:14 says that the Holy Spirit is the "down payment on our inheritance."

Meaning that the fulness of God's glorious future is ahead of us, but we've got a foretaste of it already. Some of that reality is ours right now; and not only that, it's the guarantee of the future that is to come. The Spirit within us is both the guarantee of our resurrection in the future and the means of us beginning to experience that resurrection life already.

Paul also uses the word "first fruits" when talking about the Spirit to expand on this idea. First fruits is an agricultural term— it's God's first sheaf to us of the final harvest.

He also refers to the Spirit as a "seal." In Paul's day a seal was used to make a mark on wax or clay, denoting ownership and authenticity. Followers of Jesus have been sealed with the Spirit, clearly designating them as God's people, and in Ephesians 4:30 they are "sealed for the day of redemption," once again pointing to what the future has in store for God's people, yet a future which is already operational by means of the Spirit.

All this should spell out loud and clear for us that our lives here and now ought to be something out of the ordinary; that something amazing has happened in us as individuals and as Christian communities. We participate in the very life of heaven!

Now this becomes evident in a variety of ways—in Christian worship, through spiritual gifts—but most importantly, in the day-to-day lives of Jesus-followers.

WORSHIP

When these first Jesus-followers met together to worship God, they experienced the presence and dynamic of God through the Holy Spirit amongst them in special ways. This, it seems, was both powerful and visible. From what we know, worship in these meetings was free and spontaneous, under the direction of the Spirit. From what Paul tells us in his first Corinthian letter, there was praying, singing, prophesying, and speaking in tongues. Everyone was encouraged to participate, both women and men, and all of this prompted and inspired by the Spirit. As was the orderliness and courtesy that Paul said should characterize their gatherings—properly led by the Spirit, with no one out of control. But it's clear, as New Testament scholar, Gordon Fee, points out, that the normal life of the Pauline churches was one of a "charismatic" and visible experience of the Spirit.[1]

The Spirit was present during the celebration of the Lord's Supper, the special meal that Jesus-followers shared. Paul mentions this in chapter 11 of 1 Corinthians, in a section of the letter in which he gives instruction about their worship. Sandwiched between a section on praying and prophesizing, and one on spiritual gifts, Paul takes issue with the church because of reports he has had of better-off members scoffing the food and wine to the detriment of poorer brothers and sisters. This was unacceptable. Paul tells them that they have all been baptized into one body and "made to drink of the one Spirit." When the Spirit is in control, differences in race, gender, status, and wealth melt away and everyone's contribution is to be valued.

GIFTS OF THE SPIRIT

Some of the things experienced by these early Christians were quite extraordinary and Paul calls these "gifts" or "manifestations of the Spirit." Paul lists these gifts in his letters to the Corinthians and the Romans—but it's interesting that the two lists are not

1. Fee, *God's Empowering Presence,* 894

identical, indicating that they are not necessarily comprehensive. There may be other inspired gifts that Paul does not mention— and indeed, there's no reason to suppose that there are not other "gifts" or Spirit-inspired action that might be appropriate to our day. In the context of what needed to be said to the Romans and Corinthians, Paul mentions gifts of service, miracles, and inspired utterances.

Paul, as a Jew, believed in a God who was all-powerful and was actively involved in the world. So it was natural to expect that this God, who had broken into his world through Jesus and had become a living reality in the lives of his followers, would be at work in ways that were out of the ordinary—whether through healings or through prophetic speech or through amazing, sacrificial love shown to everyone, even to enemies or the most seemingly undeserving.

God's gracious gifts of the Spirit were meant to build up the church community and to enable it to be a means of demonstrating God's love to the world.

One of the Spirit gifts that Paul highlights is that of prophecy—God-inspired messages that are meant to build up the church. When we consider prophecy in the light of the rest of scripture, it applies to more than simply the church. The Old Testament prophets were those that spoke truth to power, who raised their voices for those who were poor and disadvantaged, and who were taken advantage of by wealthy people in positions of power.

God's call to his people is that they be prophetic to their generation—providing a powerful demonstration of an alternative, loving way of life and, in the line of Israel's prophets of old, speaking truth to power. Our voices, and our very way of life, both individually and together, need to be prophetic. Too often though, our voices are raised simply to support the status quo. It's comfortable for many of us for systems of disadvantage and oppression to continue without change.

Being prophetic, however, is the way of the Spirit. That can get us into trouble at times, it can get people's backs up, but when we allow the Spirit to move, then prophetic speech and prophetic action is the natural result.

THE SPIRIT-FILLED LIFE

Paul talks in some length about the way in which the Spirit transforms the lives of Jesus-followers in his letter to the Romans when he compares life in the flesh to life in the Spirit. Life in the flesh is the old, former way of life, characterized in Romans 5 by sin and death, as opposed to the new life which believers have been given in Christ.

In Romans 8, Paul says that in the old era, the former life of the flesh, it is "impossible to please God," but that the new age of the Spirit sets us free from sin and death.

And note that Paul tells the Romans categorically that "you are not in the flesh; you are in the Spirit, if the Spirit of God lives in you." This gets pretty exciting in this passage, actually, because Paul says that it's the same Spirit that raised Christ from the dead that indwells us.

So how can things not be different? This is the new creation that Paul talks about in 2 Corinthians. And if you go to his letter to the Galatians, you'll find Paul talking about walking or living in the Spirit, and so "not fulfilling the desire of the flesh." He contrasts the life of the flesh, with its sexual immorality, idolatry, bickering and fighting, and hard partying, with the transformed life of the Spirit where new "fruit" naturally grows—love, joy, peace, patience, kindness, generosity, faithfulness, gentleness, and self-control. This beautiful way of life is the result of the death of the old way of life—being "crucified with Christ" and being resurrected into new life, animated by the powerful Spirit of God.

Paul, you see, understands the life of the Spirit by means of his Old Testament scriptures. When he read Ezekiel's vision of the valley of the dry bones, where the life-giving Spirit of God brought a bunch of desiccated bones to life, he saw that this was what was happening right before his eyes in the resurrection of Christ, and in the Spirit-life now breathed into Jesus-followers.

"I will put my Spirit within you and you shall live" from Ezekiel 37 reverberates behind Romans 8:11: "he who raised Christ from the dead will give life to your mortal bodies also through his Spirit that dwells in you."

And Jeremiah's prophesy of God's covenant written on the hearts of his people, where "new and right desires" would be a natural way of life, is clearly in Paul's mind. The letter of Christ is written in our hearts by the Holy Spirit, he says in 2 Corinthians chapter 3.

Paul's sense, then, is that something real and tangible has happened to Jesus-followers. We have been given the Spirit, the Spirit lives in us, we are led by the Spirit, God's love is poured upon us by means of the Spirit, the Spirit brings us joy and life—nothing could be clearer from this deluge of references to the Spirit, than that we are people indwelt by the very presence and power of God. You can understand why Paul thinks we should be changed people, why we're no longer in slavery to sin, to a former way of life, to life in the flesh. "You are not in the flesh, you are in the spirit."

It's a common mistake to think of the second half of Romans 7 where Paul talks of a tremendous struggle going on in the Self, where it wants to please God but cannot, as characterizing the internal struggle of the Jesus-follower, half in one world and half in the other, the old life continually tugging at him or her. That view is a problem because of Paul's talk about freedom from sin in chapter 6 and his bald statements in chapter 8 that those "in the flesh" cannot please God and "but you are not in the flesh." In chapter 7, which is largely about the powerlessness of the Jewish Torah to bring salvation, Paul is explaining how life following the law in Judaism just ends in frustration. Trying to live under the law is hopeless and those that attempt it end up not doing what they know they ought to, and doing the very things they know they ought not to do.

Paul, it seems, has higher expectations of Jesus-followers than we often do of ourselves. God's power and presence is within us—the old, with the dominating power of sin over flesh, has passed away, the new has come. If we can really believe it, if we can "present ourselves to God as those who have been brought from death to life," then not letting sin "exercise dominion in your mortal bodies" becomes a glorious possibility for us. Remember, for Paul, because of Christ's resurrection, our own resurrection has already begun.

LIFE IN THE MIDST OF MESSINESS

Not that this leads Paul to any sort of triumphalism or a sense that the future had arrived fully. Paul is only too aware of human weakness: he says that God's power is made perfect in weakness: "So, I will boast all the more gladly of my weaknesses, so that the power of Christ may dwell in me" (2 Corinthians 12:9).

It's the Spirit, Paul says, in Romans 8, that helps us in our weakness. Paul knew that the Jesus-followers to whom he was writing had difficult lives, were often hungry and suffered hardship and distress—as he himself did. Suffering for Christ was to be expected, it was a privilege, and he advised the Romans to be patient in suffering.

Our culture tends to think of suffering and pain as completely unacceptable, an evil to be avoided at all costs. Paul, on the other hand, knew that life in this age would inevitably bring suffering, and said that "we boast in our suffering," and that suffering for Christ was "a privilege."

Paul knew that life's hardship and trouble would continue to be a part of believers' lives. But somehow in the midst of that hardship is the very presence of God himself—in the person of God the Spirit, indwelling Jesus-followers' lives and their community life.

Giving them the power to support each other in love, to encourage one another and to spread that love to all around.

And, in the midst of the messiness of life, to be overcomers—super-conquerors. And, amazingly, to have joy. The kingdom of God is justice, peace, and joy in the Holy Spirit.

We've seen how Paul saw the gospel as the good news of the arrival of God's loving, revolutionary kingdom, authenticated by the death and resurrection of the Messiah, where justice, peace, and joy are the hallmarks, and where Jesus-followers are to demonstrate the life of the future here and now. Now we come to see that this amazing possibility—of life in the midst of death—of joy in the midst of sorrow—of rediscovering our true humanity—is wonderfully, gloriously possible, because of this beautiful gift that God has given us—his very own power and presence in the person of the Holy Spirit.

We need to be very careful, however. This morning I read a *Christianity Today* article online. It was about an aspect of American politics. What shocked me were the responses from people who claim to be Christians on both sides of the debate. The level of vitriol and unkindness from people claiming to follow Jesus was quite dispiriting. It struck me that this is precisely the sort of behavior which could be in Paul's sights when he talks about offending the Holy Spirit. In 1 Thessalonians 5, right after he has told the Thessalonians they ought "always seek to do good to one another," Paul instructs them not to quench or stifle the Spirit. The sort of mean-spirited, unkind things I read online represent a serious stifling of the Spirit.

This sort of self-control-lacking, joyless, aggressive behavior is off the table for Jesus-followers. Offending and quenching the Spirit in this way puts our claims to follow Jesus in serious question.

The challenge to us right now is Paul's challenge to the Ephesians: Be filled with the Spirit. Let the presence and power of the Spirit, of God himself, fill you to overflowing. There's an ongoing sense to what Paul says here—this is not a one-time experience. It's a day-by-day surrender and opening up to God to allow God's presence and power to be at work in our lives.

Paul warns us not to grieve or offend the Holy Spirit by slipping into old ways of anger or dishonesty or greediness or "rotten" speech. Rather, he gives us the imperative to let God fill us with his Spirit, letting it fully sink in that God himself lives in us to enable us to live the life of the future, even now. That clearly involves mindfulness on our part each day, an opening up to God and an expectation of seeing God at work as we go about our lives and engage with other people.

Two millennia may separate us from those first Christians; but the same Spirit who raised Christ from the dead gives life to us. Dare we believe that? Can we let the Spirit of God, the presence of God, fill us and fill our churches, and blow away the cobwebs of unbelief, insipidness, and ordinariness? Can we follow the Spirit's lead to fight for justice, to raise our voices for the powerless, and to care for those in need?

Be filled and go on being filled with the Spirit!

REFLECTION

Does Paul put more emphasis on the working of the Spirit than we do in our churches?

How relevant today is the picture of the meetings of the early Christians being lively affairs with everybody invited to participate? Does my life / church have a "charismatic" dimension? Should we expect it to be the same as 2,000 years ago, or is it different for our time?

Are we too pessimistic about the possibilities for being "freed from sin?"

How does the Spirit help us in times of hardship and difficulty?

What does "being filled with the Spirit" mean on a daily basis?

If we believe *our lives here and now ought to be something out of the ordinary* in what way should they be more than merely different, but exceptional? How does this tie in with the fruits of the Spirit?

FURTHER READING

John R. Levison, *Fresh Air: The Holy Spirit for an Inspired Life*, Paraclete Press, 2012.
Gordon Fee, *Paul, the Spirit and the People of God*, Hendrickson, 1994.

7

Jesus, the World's One True Lord

JESUS IS LORD

As we're discovering, Paul said some pretty outrageous things. Perhaps one of the most outrageous and far-fetched things he said was that the Jewish man, Jesus, who had been ignominiously executed by the Romans, hanging naked on a cross, was now the complete master and ruler of the universe! Jesus, he said, was Lord.

To his Jewish compatriots, this was scandalous and the idea of someone who had been deemed cursed by the Torah because of the method of his death becoming exalted in such a way was unthinkable. To the pagans Paul met, the idea was ludicrous. Everyone knew there were a myriad of gods who might be deemed "lord" in some way and talk of one supreme god—in fact, only one God—who alone was worthy of worship and allegiance was so much stuff and nonsense. On top of that, the peoples of the empire knew the true reality of the world—that Caesar was Lord. He was the one whose rule and diktats governed their lives, and what's more, Caesar needed that to be acknowledged.

Paul's idea about Jesus being Lord was outrageous then; and it's outrageous now. Try telling anyone today that Jesus is the world's true governor and ruler, and that he demands complete allegiance beyond country, family or even one's self, and they'll think you're a religious nutcase. And probably a dangerous one, as well.

THE HIGHEST POSITION

For Paul, the fact that God had raised Jesus from the dead meant that Jesus was Lord. He explains to the Philippians that because of Jesus's faithfulness and humility in subjecting himself to the cross, God "has highly exalted him," meaning God had exalted him to the highest possible degree. God raised him from the dead and "gave him a name above every name" such that everyone will eventually acknowledge that "Jesus is Lord."

As Gordon Fee argues, what Paul is saying here is that God attributed to Jesus *the* name above every name—that is, the Divine Name from Paul's scriptures.[1] This is the highest name in the universe. What Paul is arguing here is quite breath-taking, and when he goes on to say that every knee will bow to this name, he is quoting Isaiah 45:23 directly. The passage in Isaiah speaks of Israel's God, Yahweh, as Savior and only God, to whom alone obeisance is required. All of that, according to Paul, is now to be ascribed to Jesus, upon his resurrection and ascension.

Every tongue would confess this at last, says Paul, meaning that now that Jesus is risen, this Lord will have the last say, and that the power of every government, ruler, tyrant, and king, and every demonic power at work in the work is only transitory, and is answerable to the Lord Christ.

This attribution of the word "Lord" to Jesus is everywhere in Paul. It's the way that he thinks now about the world. Everything is relative to this: Jesus is Lord.

In Romans 10:9, Paul makes the connection between the resurrection and the Lordship of Jesus crystal clear: "If you confess with your lips that Jesus is Lord and believe in your heart that God

---

1. Fee, *Pauline Christology*, 396–398

raised him from the dead, you will be saved." In this passage, Paul again uses one of the scriptures of Israel which refers to Yahweh and attributes it to Jesus—"everyone who calls on the name of the LORD shall be saved" (Joel 2:32). When we add Romans 1:4 to the mix, there's no doubt about what Paul thought about Jesus. Jesus, he said, had been declared the Son of God with power and as Lord "by the resurrection from the dead."

Because of the resurrection, Jesus has ascended and taken his place at the highest position in the cosmos. When you think about it, we're in pretty heady territory here, aren't we? Most people have no problem with Jesus as a good person, as a wise teacher, but when we start to claim, first of all that his corpse stood up, alive and transformed, and then that this human being is now running the universe and demands our allegiance, many people start to get a bit uncomfortable.

So, what does it mean to say that Jesus is Lord? And is it good news?

THE POWERS THAT HOLD HUMANITY CAPTIVE

The world in which Paul lived was full of religious cults, gods, goddesses and superstition. Gods needed to be honored and placated if the forces of chaos in neighborhood and family were to be avoided. Often the word "lord" was used to speak of the god or goddess of various cults. The world was seen as the domain of a myriad of malign forces that exercised power over individuals and communities.

Paul's view of the variety of gods worshiped in his world was that they were simply "so-called gods," and the true Lord, "through whom are all things and through whom we exist" (1 Corinthians 8:5—6), was Jesus the Messiah. He agreed, however, that there were suprahuman powers at work in the world, what he called the "fundamental elements" that held human beings captive.

In his letters, Paul refers to a variety of "powers" at work in the world. These include principalities and powers, rulers, authorities, thrones, and dominions. Some of these are clearly human, as in Romans 13:1—7, others are spiritual, and sometimes Paul is ambiguous and is probably lumping all powers together, earthly and heavenly.

In Ephesians 2, Paul refers to "the power of the air, the spirit now at work among those who are disobedient." Paul here is aware of the fact of evil at work in the world, which leaves us "dead in our trespasses and sins." But this "spirit now at work," we might view as the deadly godless atmosphere of the world which we breath and then pass on like a virus through our individual actions, and the cultural, political, and institutional structures which have fallen prey to violent and oppressive ways of operating.

Paul has a pretty dark view of a world which needs rescuing by God. It's a world which has fallen in thrall to sinister cosmic powers, which oppose God's purposes, and oppress and dehumanize people.

We see this dark picture of humanity's plight emerging throughout his writing, especially when he writes about sin. In Romans 6, he sees refers to Sin as a power, a ruthless slave master, which controls people's behavior. There's a vicious circle, explains Paul in Romans 5—Adam by his disobedience introduced sin into the world, and all of us who follow after commit sin, thus, it seems, giving Sin power over human beings. In Romans 7, not even the Jewish Law can withstand the influence of Sin, and in Galatians 5, Paul refers to Sin directly as a controlling power.

It's easy to see this nexus of the power of Sin and human compliance when we think of, say, racism or war. When a society has a history of oppressing one group of people because of the color of their skin, a whole way of thinking begins to take hold which becomes dominant and, perhaps for a long time, insidiously embedded in the way of life of a whole population. So there is an institutionalized, embedded racism, a power, if you like, which holds people in thrall, causing them to act in ways that discriminate and oppress others. This can in no way absolve individuals of their own responsibility to act in just ways, but it indicates the way in which the power of Sin is at work in the world.

Similarly, with war—today I read of two soldiers, army privates, from Myanmar who were testifying to the Hague about the genocide their army had carried out against the Rohingya people in their country. These soldiers had themselves committed terrible atrocities under the orders and, presumably, pain of death from their officers. Again, we see the actions of individuals—yes, sinning in the most heinous way and accountable for their actions, but under the coercion of powers beyond them, this time earthly powers. And yet earthly powers that can be traced again to an historical legacy that grips this country, a spiritual power.

But it is clear that Paul sees every power as firmly under the lordship of the risen and exalted Jesus. In Ephesians 1, Christ is "far above all rule and authority and power and dominion." This is not just something for the future—for Paul, this is a reality now. For Paul and the first Christians, this could be seen amongst them by the sick being healed, demons being cast out, their release from addictive and sinful behaviors, and the reality of a new peaceful and loving environment within the Jesus community, where the oppressive hierarchies of the empire were negated.

In their personal and community lives, Jesus's defeat of the powers was a tangible reality. Paul sees every malevolent, enslaving power as now having been defeated by the death, resurrection, and ascension of Jesus. The good news of the gospel is that the resurrection of Christ and the Lordship of Jesus means that all these powers have been dethroned. Paul paints a graphic picture of this in Colossians 2: "God disarmed the rulers and authorities and made a public example of them, triumphing over them in it." Here he has in mind the victory parade of the returning Roman general, who has his war booty, disgraced and in chains, trailing behind him.

For Jews who were frustrated by the Law's power to help them obey God ("For I do not do the good I want, but the evil I do not want is what I do" (Romans 7:19)); and for pagans who felt their lives were controlled by the forces of chaos, the Lordship of Jesus meant freedom. Paul said that Jesus-followers were now free from the power of Sin and were now able to choose to obey God.

They were now "in the Spirit" which made it possible to live in a way which pleased God. In addition, they need not now fear that malign spiritual powers would bring disaster to their lives.

The lordship of Jesus means freedom for us as well. There really can be freedom from the inauthentic lives we may have lived in the past; from addictive behavior; from slavish conformity to the inhuman forces of consumerism, self-promotion, and unjust and domineering conduct; from unhealthy and selfish sexual activity—in short from sin. "Sin," says Paul quite bluntly, "shall not be master over you."

The good news of the gospel is that there is freedom to be part of God's new creation, where there is love, light, and joy. Things can be different for each one of us, because Jesus is Lord.

HUMAN POWERS

Paul's language of power includes not only spiritual powers but human powers. The Lordship of Jesus is total—not only over spiritual powers but over every earthly authority as well.

Paul's gospel, as we have seen, was about the coming of God to reclaim his world, it was about the kingdom of God, it was about who was the true ruler of the world. That being the case, it must in some sense have been quite subversive to the Roman Empire in which he lived.

Rome was an oppressive, violent, and domineering force in the lives of the peoples of the empire. The Roman emperor was proclaimed and honoured as divine. He was promoted as the "savior," who was guided and blessed by the gods, who gave him military victory and the ability to subdue and dominate other people groups. His propaganda said that he brought "peace" to the world—by the required level of violence of course.

Nero, for example, the emperor in power when Paul wrote his letter to the Romans, was a tyrant who exhibited astounding extravagance and was known for spectacular violence. But he was hailed as "the lord of the whole world," "the source of all things," "the only one from the beginning of time." He was called "lord" and "saviour of the world."

In Paul's day, the cult of Caesar in which the Roman emperor was proclaimed and honoured as divine was the fastest growing religion in the empire. Day by day Jesus-followers were exposed to and surrounded by the images and message of Caesar and the empire in the architecture, statues, temples, coinage, and festivals, all extolling the virtue of Rome and its rulers. The word "gospel" was typically used of Caesar, the emperor, celebrating his birth or accession to the throne.

Against all this, Paul stands in the Jewish tradition of seeing Gentile rulers and their kingdoms as God's servants, where God raises up rulers and tears them down at his will. Paul's gospel, which was in effect a call to allegiance to another king (Acts 16: 20-21), got him into trouble in the Roman colony of Philippi where he ended up in jail. And, of course, he eventually was brought to Rome where he was executed by the Roman regime.

Paul's gospel was that Jesus was the world's true Lord, whose kingly rule had now come. That was not a message welcome to the ears of a world power that demanded complete allegiance from its citizens.

In the centre of an empire that proclaimed its accomplishments of world domination by military might, severe taxation, and ruthless enforcement as the Pax Romana, "peace"—Paul speaks of an alternative reality, that of a world which is ruled by God, to whom the Roman emperors must answer and who brings to the world a true and just peace.

In Romans 13:1—7, Paul makes it clear that the Roman authorities have been instituted by, and are the servants of, his Jewish God. Not a message that would have warmed Nero's heart. For sure, Paul is not advocating civil anarchy in this passage, but a close look shows that while Paul offers sensible advice to a small, vulnerable group in the heart of the empire, he limits and relativizes human governments. They are necessary and have a job to do—but they answer to God. Ultimately, the world's true Lord is Jesus.

Paul's view, expressed here and in passages like Colossians 1 and 1 Timothy 2, is that the powers on earth and in heaven are created by God and are to play their role in the structure of God's world. But at the same time, they are subservient to God and, with the advent of the Messiah, a new sort of rulership was being announced which called for the allegiance of all.

The problem for Jesus-followers in the cities of the Roman Empire to whom Paul wrote was that the dominant power of the day positioned itself, with divine pretensions, as the place where justice and peace were to found, and demanded the absolute loyalty of its citizens.

And clearly, in our world, where tyrants and strong men exert their violent rule, we can understand how worldly powers can be said to have been co-opted by negative spiritual forces. A quick consideration of Nazi Germany or Pol Pot's Cambodia or any other heinous regimes we might mention should leave us in no doubt as to the potential for abusive, godless governments to hold large populations captive physically, mentally, and spiritually.

But even those of us who live in the liberal democracies of the twenty-first century ought to be wary of the way in which governments and political ideologies vie for our allegiance. Where it becomes the norm and somehow integrated within our Christian faith to give blind obedience to the flag, the military, and "our way of life." The idea of "Christian nationalism" is actually an oxymoron—unwavering allegiance to our particular nation puts us right out of kilter with the Lordship of Jesus.

The fact of Jesus's Lordship means that any authority that exists is subject to his authority. Jesus-followers first and foremost follow Jesus in the way of sacrificial love, love of enemies, and peace. That will inevitably put us at odds with the economics-driven, militaristic, and life-sapping power of even our liberal democracy. Add in the rejection of truth that has become part of modern political operations and we need to be very careful about how far our national allegiance takes us.

Paul never advocates anarchy; he wants us to pray for those in authority so they might keep the forces of chaos at bay to enable people to live a "quiet and peaceable life in all . . . dignity" (1 Timothy 2:1—2). But Christ is now the "head of all rule and authority" (Colossians 2:10). Every human authority is subject to him and our allegiance is first and foremost to him.

DEATH—THE FINAL ENEMY

For Paul, the ultimate power at work in the world is that of death. This age, he says, in Romans 5, is dominated by sin and death. It's the "final enemy" which Christ will destroy before "handing over the kingdom to God the Father." This enemy, which all of us must face, has been defeated already by Jesus—he has already burst through this power and broken its sting for all of us: "Death has been swallowed up in victory. Where, O death, is your victory? Where, O death, is your sting?" (1 Corinthians 15:54—55).

The resurrection of Jesus, for Paul, was the first of the general resurrection at the end of the age. The fact of his resurrection is the absolute guarantee that all those who own allegiance to him, who are "in Christ" will themselves be resurrected to take their place in the new, restored kingdom over which Jesus will rule, on that day when every knee will bow and every tongue confess that he is Lord.

LIVING UNDER JESUS'S LORDSHIP

Paul is convinced that the death and resurrection of Jesus has inexorably changed the world. The resurrection and the ascension of Jesus to the highest place in the universe at "the right hand of God" means that the enslaving potency of every power has been utterly broken. Every power and authority, whether human or spiritual, is now subject to Jesus. We asked earlier whether the Lordship of Christ was good news. And now we see that it absolutely is!

When we say that Jesus is Lord, it means that:

- Sin no longer has to be a way of life for us. Jesus has liberated us from its power, however that affects us, whether through ingrained habitual practices, our own selfishness or through the social pressure to be conformed to consumerism, racism, sexism or any other sort of -ism.

- We have been released from every spiritual power that might oppose us or hold us down in any way.

- We are free to love God, living lives of joyful service, without the constraining bonds of self-centredness.

- Every tyrant and godless, oppressive regime is under notice that its day is limited and it will have its come-uppance in the final day of God's justice, if not before.

- We are called to give our primary allegiance to the Lord Jesus and the values of his kingdom—love, peace, non-violence— to the exclusion of all other competing claims that do not conform to these, including those from governments or any other earthly authority.

And it means that the last, dark power that hovers over our lives—death—has been utterly defeated and will not have the ultimate claim over us. This gives a freedom and a joy to our lives now which liberates us to live in a way that witnesses to Jesus's Lordship and challenges every power, human or spiritual, that sets itself against his loving, peaceful kingdom.

Jesus is Lord means that we are free to live authentically human lives, free from everything that would hold us back. The question is: are we prepared, now, in every aspect of our lives, to fully bow the knee and confess that Jesus is Lord, to the glory of God the Father?

REFLECTION

In what ways can we see sin as a controlling power? In our own lives; in the wider world?

How does Jesus set us free?

Is Paul's view of "spiritual" powers simply part of his first century culture? How relevant is it to our modern world?

In way ways can we see spiritual powers at work in our world?

If "Jesus is Lord, not Caesar," what does that mean for the way we see our relationship to the government and power structures under which we live?

In the list of effects of the Lordship of Jesus given towards the end of the chapter, which for you are the most challenging?

How important is it to know that Jesus has conquered death?

FURTHER READING

Gary W. Burnett, *The Gospel According to the Blues,* Cascade, 2014, Chapter 7.

Gordon D. Fee, *Pauline Christology*, Hendrickson, 2007.

Walter Wink, *Naming the Powers: The Language of Power in the New Testament,* Fortress, 1984.

N.T. Wright, *Evil and the Justice of God*, SPCK, 2006.

8

Being the Justice of God in the World

GOD'S JUSTICE PROJECT

WE'VE BEEN TALKING so far about the broad contours of Paul's gospel which was all about Jesus and the love of God, about the significance of Jesus's death and resurrection, about Jesus reigning as king, and about God's intention to transform the world. And about how we are involved in that fantastic project.

Now we want to have a look at how Paul saw all this playing out in the world. The first thing to look at is how the gospel brings God's justice—God's plan to make things right in the world.

When I was a boy, I always wanted to stay up late on a Saturday evening to watch Match of the Day, the round-up of the day's football, but was seldom allowed. "It's not fair!" I'd cry. As children we have what seems to be an in-built sense of what's fair and equitable, and it's the cause of countless siblings' quarrels. But that sense of needing justice is something that never really goes away and most of us want what's right, just, and fair. We yearn for Rev.

Martin Luther King Jr.'s words to be true when he said, "The arc of the moral universe is long, but it bends toward justice."

Paul's Jewish tradition had a strong sense of God as a God of justice. The Psalmist says again and again, that God "judges the peoples with equity," and that God "sought justice for the orphan and the oppressed, and upheld the cause of the lowly and destitute." The prophets railed against the exploitation of the poor by the wealthy and powerful, and cried out for justice to "roll down like waters." And Paul was aware of Micah's view of God's requirement of humanity "to do justice, to love kindness, and to walk humbly with your God."

So, we might well expect justice to be a big part of what Paul saw God doing in the world through Jesus the Messiah—putting things right, making things fair and just. The gospel tells of God's amazing love for the world and his coming to take charge of things. Fundamentally this is God's justice project.

And, not surprisingly, we find Paul talking time and time again about God's justice and God making things right—he uses words associated with this well over a hundred times. It's in the good news about Jesus the Messiah that the "saving justice" of God is revealed. This "making right" by God is what God does for people who trust in and follow Jesus—God justifies them, and this is entirely brought about by the faithfulness of Jesus the Messiah (Romans 3:22).

We've already thought about how the death and resurrection of Jesus deals with our sin, and how the transformational power of being "in Christ" and of the Holy Spirit can change individuals and make us living demonstrations of God's in-breaking kingdom. Justification, that great Pauline doctrine that many people think of the moment Paul is mentioned, is about far more than being acquitted in God's courtroom. As New Testament scholar, Michael Gorman puts it, "Justification means that the unjust are being liberated from injustice to live justly."

Gorman's insightful paraphrase of Romans 5:8 helps make this clear: "But God demonstrates his kind of justice and his love for us in that while we were unjust toward others and unloving toward God, Christ died for us to restore us to justice and love."[1]

God's saving justice is all about God making things right in his world—something which God will do eventually and fully at the return of Christ, but which God has already begun through those he has already set right. God's justice project has begun, and we are a part of it!

THE GREAT EXCHANGE

Paul was the founder of the small Christian group in the city of Corinth. The city was a Roman colony and the church was made up mainly of people who had come to faith from a pagan background. Paul felt a great deal of affection for these believers, but, as we read the two letters we have, it seems he was terribly anxious about some of the reports he had been getting about the church.

In his first letter, he tries to put them straight on a whole range of matters from divisions amongst them to sexual immorality to disorder in their meetings to abuse of poorer members of the congregation at the Lord's Supper. Coming from a pagan background, the Corinthians had a hard time really grasping some basic elements of Christian faith and so Paul writes to help them back on the right track.

In Paul's second letter to Corinth, some time has passed and the situation is that the Corinthians have been visited by some other Christian missionaries who seemingly have scant regard for Paul, and Paul finds himself having to defend himself. And as the letter goes on, Paul gets more and more hot under the collar about these people, referring to them very sarcastically as "super-apostles."

So, in the first few chapters of his second letter, we have Paul talking about the relationship he's had with the Corinthians, stressing all the ways that he and his colleagues have been faithful ministers of Christ, seeking to serve and love the Corinthians. In chapter 5 of the letter, this defence of his own ministry continues. Paul is

---

1. Gorman, *Becoming the Gospel*, 227, 232

defending his and his colleagues' divinely-appointed credentials as ambassadors to the Corinthians, in the face of the nay-saying of other opposing Christian leaders. As we read on in chapter 6, Paul continues in this vein, showing that he and his friends are the true servants of God.

So, throughout this whole section of the letter, we have Paul vigorously defending himself over against the attack and bad-mouthing of another group of Christian leaders. So, if *this* is what chapters 5 and 6 of the letter are about—what then, is happening in verse 21 of chapter 5 when Paul says, "God made him who had no sin to be sin for us, so that in him we might become the righteousness of God"?

This verse is often talked about as "the great exchange." Christ takes on our sin and we take on his righteousness. It's like an exchange of clothes or coats. Christ takes our dirty old coat of sin, puts it on, and in exchange gives us a new coat of righteousness. So, we get his goodness, his perfection, and he takes our sin.

Except . . . I'm not sure that this explanation of the verse fits the context very well. Paul is defending carefully and strongly, right up to verse 20 of chapter 5, his own apostleship and then goes on with this defense in chapter 6—so can he *really* be veering off here at such a tangent?

BEING THE JUSTICE OF GOD

Once we look carefully at the context of the whole passage, I think we are forced to think again about what Paul might be saying here. And there might *just* might be a better way to interpret the verse.

Let's think about this phrase "the righteousness of God," which is a favourite of Paul's. And as well as this phrase, Paul uses other related Greek words very, very frequently in his letters— words that we variously translate as just, justice, justified, or right, righteousness, righteous. The fact of the matter is, there is a whole family of Greek words which have the same root, but which, in our rich English language, we can translate in two different ways. We either use our English Anglo-Saxon background which gives us the words "make right, righteous, righteousness," or we can use our Latin background and use words like "justify, just, and justice." But it's the same basic Greek word group that Paul is using.

All of which muddies the waters when we come to understanding Paul. Righteousness is a perfectly correct translation, but for us, righteousness language has come to have certain religious, churchy overtones and maybe doesn't help us get to grips with what Paul is saying.

But we have the option of using the *justice* group of words in this verse which maybe gives us a better sense of what Paul means. That we might become the "justice of God."

With this translation we start to think of God's action to make things just, to make things right. That's what's needed in the world, fallen and bent out of shape—it needs God to come and fix things, including us, to put things right, to bring his justice. And that, of course, is exactly what God has done in Christ—God has acted to deal with the power of sin and evil, which Christ took upon himself and exhausted so that God might once more reign over his world and begin the process of transformation, reconciliation, and justice.

This is what Paul refers to in Romans 1:17—"I am convinced," he says, "that in the gospel of Jesus the Messiah, the justice of God is revealed"—it's in *this* way that God's rectifying, justice-bringing, world-transforming work has been done.

It's in the death and resurrection of Christ that God's justice is revealed—this is how God's world-transforming and salvation project comes to realization. This is the righteousness of God; this is the justice of God. As we've seen, through Christ's death and resurrection, God has reclaimed God's world. God has begun the process of world transformation, which will be completed when Jesus returns. The righteousness or the justice of God is all about God putting things right in God's world, setting individuals right and bringing justice to the world.

In using the phrase, the righteousness of God, Paul is taking his cue from his Jewish scriptures where the sense is that of the saving, faithful action of the creator and covenant God in the world, bringing his justice and peace, and applying that to what God has done in Christ.

Now once we start to see the phrase in this light, then the problems we began to see with how the verse at 5:21 fits in with everything before and everything after begin to disappear.

So, now we might read our verse like this: "For our sake, God made Christ to be sin, who, of course, himself knew no sin, so that in him we might become the saving action, the justice of God in the world."

What Paul is saying here is this: God was in the Messiah, Jesus, reconciling the world to himself. He's given that message to us, his ambassadors, so that we might appeal to the world on his behalf. Actually, God made Christ to be sin—that is, to stand in our place, taking on himself our sin, our unjust actions, so that we might stand in his place, doing what Jesus was doing—being the justice of God in the world.

When Paul says that we have become the righteousness or justice of God, he's pointing to our mission in the purposes of God. A great exchange has taken place all right, but perhaps not in the way we've previously thought of it. Our way of life, of self-centeredness, of self-promotion, of injustice, has been taken and dealt with by Christ—a whole orientation of life that negates the image of God that we were supposed to be. And now we are free to fulfill our human calling—to be God's image, to reflect what God is, to be God's saving justice to the world. Just as Christ was the righteousness, the justice of God, so we, too, being "in Christ," are called to reflect and to be that justice.

I BELIEVE THERE'S A BETTER DAY

And that's what these little groups of Jesus-followers did. In a very hierarchical world, where status meant a great deal, where you didn't associate with people you thought of as lower than you, where people were largely left to fend for themselves, Christians created new, just communities, where people like Sabina the day-laborer and Primus the slave were welcomed and accepted.

There was no slave or free; there was no difference between Jew or Gentile; women could participate on equal terms with men. They modelled a new, just way of being.

Paul shows us one way in which this was worked out in a couple of later chapters in this second letter to the Corinthians. In chapters 8 and 9, he appeals to them to support his collection of funds for poor Jesus-followers in Jerusalem, an appeal that New Testament scholar, Katherine Grieb, says is founded on "the generous justice of God."[2] Paul wanted there to be economic justice between the Christian communities, based on the generosity of those who had more, as a direct outflow of the change that God had made in their lives, transforming them into people who lived justly.

And we too are called to live out the great exchange of the cross. We can and ought to be doing that in our Christian communities. Our "heavenly citizenship," as Paul puts it, is to be reflected in our life together. Where people from diverse backgrounds, races, and ethnic groups can come together in harmony, sharing their lives, learning from each other and supporting each other in a myriad of ways, including financially.

But we have an opportunity that those early Christians didn't have—they lived under a brutal military regime where agitating for political change was impossible. We, on the other hand, do have the opportunity to challenge the injustice we see around us in the world, whether that's hunger or human trafficking or economic inequality, sexism, or racism. God's call is for us to be God's justice in the world—to live in our communities and with the wider world as those who are anticipating the peaceful, just reign of God in the world.

Jesus taught us to pray, "your kingdom come on earth as it is in heaven." We are both to pray for the kingdom *and* to orientate our lives to this vision, and so to bear witness to the loving, justice of God.

For Christ to be the justice of God, it took everything. It led him to suffering, it led him to the cross. What might it take for us

2. Quoted in *Gorman, Becoming the Gospel*, 252

to be the justice of God in the world? Standing up in order to make things right is rarely easy, whether it's:

- simply not laughing at a sexist joke at work, or, maybe even in a church context, or calling out racism when we see it, or

- deciding not to take this particular piece of business because it deals with a company whose products or practices perpetuate some injustice, or a regime that abuses human rights, or

- deciding not to spend money on ourselves in the way that everybody else does—"hey, it's the latest bit of technology, everybody's got it, I need it"—because we have better ways to use our money to bless others, or

- not giving our heart and soul and all the hours God gives to our work, because we have family who depend on us and a whole world that needs us, or

- finally deciding to get involved in some organization which is working to bring God's loving justice in some way, or

- finding ways to live more simply so as to contribute less to climate change which is destroying the planet and having a devastating effect on poor communities around the world, or

- making our voice heard on behalf of the oppressed, the powerless and those suffering injustice by lobbying those in power and, when needed, in peaceful protest.

All of this, and many other things the Holy Spirit might remind you of, needs us to begin to imagine a different, more just world and the part we can play in seeking that.

There *is* a better day coming—God's final day of justice, peace, and equity. But we need to lift our eyes beyond the injustice and oppression and inequity that characterizes our world and begin to imagine some of God's new world into the present one and to live lives that reflect that.

Our challenge, in the face of temptation and the pull of selfishness, and in the face of tyrants and empires, and the advertising industry, and wasting time in front of the TV, is to live in a way that anticipates and demonstrates the justice of God to a needy world. Both in the way we live together in our Christian communities and in the way in which we seek justice in the wider world. We cannot afford simply to be content with a status quo that perpetuates inequity and any level of oppression.

This is our calling, this our mission—to be the justice of God. That needs to grip us and transform us, so that we, in turn, might begin to transform the world, "to become the justice of God in the world."

REFLECTION

What does the Old Testament tell us about God's commitment to the poor and marginalized?

In what ways did Jesus reflect God's commitment to justice?

How does a translation of "justice" rather than "righteousness" affect our understanding of what Paul has to say?

How can our church community better reflect a new, just world? Consider individual actions and ones that might require working together.

What practical ways can we live more justly?

Consider the support we might need if we begin to face up to injustice.

FURTHER READING

Michael J. Gorman, *Becoming the Gospel: Paul, Participation, and Mission, (in italics)* Eerdmans, 2015, esp. chapter 7.

N.T. Wright, "On becoming the righteousness of God," in D.M. Hay (ed.), *Pauline Theology, Volume II*, Fortress, 1993.

J.D.G Dunn & Alan M. Suggate, *The Justice of God: A Fresh Look at the Old Doctrine of Justification by Faith*, Eerdmans, 1994.

Nicholas Wolterstorff, *Justice in Love*, Eerdmans, 2011.

9

Radical Peacefulness

REVENGE IS SWEET

REVENGE IS SWEET. REVENGE is a dish best served cold. From the sack of Troy in Homer's Iliad to modern Sicilian blood feuds to acts of revenge by the military and intelligence services of modern nations to petty grievances within families, revenge and violence against those we feel have wronged us is pretty much built in to the fabric of life.

And it's reinforced by the plot line of innumerable movies and television shows, where we cheer on retribution against those who have wronged the hero. The bad guys use violence to get what they want and the good guys then need to defend themselves using violence. A typical story line in the movies and TV we watch sees the good guy going after the criminals at great personal cost, in the end getting the job done—of course—but along the way leaving a bloody trail of mayhem, explosions, and shot-up bad guys. Well, that's what's needed, right?

The myth of redemptive violence. That's how theologian Walter Wink describes the paradigm which is reinforced in popular entertainment but which also underpins the very fabric of the modern nation-state. Wink says this is "the real myth of the modern world . . . the dominant religion in our society today," which results in a view that violence in itself is not wrong, it is simply a fact—the social order depends critically on violence to suppress the powers of disorder.[1]

PAUL'S RADICAL PEACEFULNESS

The New Testament runs completely counter to this way of thinking. It's so out-of-sync with the way our world, including we ourselves, have come to think, that the teaching of Jesus and that of Paul, his disciple, are often largely ignored by those of us who think of ourselves as Christian.

So here we come to another of those outrageous things that Paul said in his letters. In Romans 12, he says: "Beloved, never seek revenge. Repay no one evil for evil."

On the contrary, "If your enemy is hungry, feed him; if he is thirsty, give him something to drink."

But Paul, you don't know the awful things they've done to me, to my country, to my community. And, you, you're just a preacher, what do you know about this?

To which Paul might say, "You do know, that they've thrown me in prison several times, which was pretty rough, to say the least; I've been harassed, cursed, mocked, ostracized by my own people. They even tried to stone me once.

"And five times—five times, they gave me thirty-nine lashes. Have you any idea what that was like? Your back ends up in pulp. And afterwards is almost as bad as the whipping, when your friends clean your wounds and put salt into them.

"The last time, I remember thinking—just for a moment—about when I was younger and had my mates with me, and we went round trying to teach those very first Jesus-followers in Judaea as brutal a lesson as we could—and if I had those lads with me, I'd get even for this lashing.

---

1. Wink, "Facing the Myth of Redemptive Violence."

"But that was just for a moment. I began to think of Jesus, who went as a lamb to the slaughter, who didn't open his mouth, who loved me and died for me. And I remembered what I'd been taught he'd said, "Do not resist the one who is evil. But if anyone slaps you on the right cheek, turn to him the other also. You have heard that it was said, "You shall love your neighbor and hate your enemy." But I say to you, Love your enemies and pray for those who persecute you."

"And so I asked God's forgiveness and I began to pray for them."

Paul, more than any of us, knew what being treated badly meant. And yet he says, along with Jesus, never seek revenge. On the contrary, seek the good of your enemy.

GOD'S PEACEFUL KINGDOM

Now that is radical! That is what the kingdom of God looks like. We've been looking at the gospel Paul preached, how it was centred around the Lordship of Christ, that it was the same gospel that Jesus preached, that it was all about the arrival of the kingdom or rule of God. And how the Jesus-followers in the first century, even though their lives were difficult, formed communities that lived out the radical love of God's kingdom and showed their world the sort of transformation that God wanted to bring.

This gospel of Jesus Christ, this kingdom of God, isn't safe, it isn't cosy. It's something that breaks apart the world as we know it and says that something greater and better and extraordinary has arrived. And it's incomprehensible to the world as we know it, because it's made of love—for everyone, including enemies. And that's what we as Jesus-followers are called to.

It's a radical kingdom of peace. In Romans 14, Paul says that the kingdom of God consists of justice, peace, and joy in the Holy Spirit. We've already talked about the justice that is at the heart of the gospel and the dynamic power of the Spirit let loose in our lives and the world. But let's think about peace.

What is the phrase Paul most often uses when he's talking about God? Is it God of truth, God of hope, God of wrath or God of love? The phrase Paul most uses most, actually, is *God of peace*. Peace is at the core of God's being. And it's at the core of Paul's theology.

As we've already seen, Paul was a Jew, a Pharisee, shaped and molded by his tradition and his scriptures. And the idea of peace—shalom—is very important in the Old Testament. Shalom is a big concept—it's about wholeness, health, security, well-being. And it's what God desires for his people and for God's world. Shalom is the result of the justice of God coming and the enjoyment of that by God's people. Paul's expectation was that peace would be a key element of the good news of Jesus the Messiah.

This, of course, includes "peace in your heart"—the sense of inward peace that comes with an experience of God's incredible love and God's forgiveness. But there is much more involved here—peaceful relations between people and peace-making are key components of the New Testament idea of peace.

The word shalom occurs frequently in Paul's scriptures (our Old Testament)—over 150 times, and is all about the flourishing of God's creation. Ultimately there was a hope for a lasting, permanent peace where nations would "beat their swords into plowshares," where they would "learn war no more" (Isaiah 2:4), and where "violence shall no more be heard in your land" (Isaiah 60:18).

God's covenant (the way in which God bound himself to his people) was to be a covenant of peace. The prophets spoke of a new day when God would renew the covenant with his people and it would be a covenant of peace. Look through Ezekiel, and especially Isaiah, and see how many times God promises his people that God will make a covenant of peace. In chapter 37 of Ezekiel, God says,

> I will make a covenant of peace with them; it shall be an everlasting covenant with them; and I will bless them and multiply them, and will set my sanctuary among them forevermore.

These were texts that came to be read by Jews as an expectation of a future messianic age of peace, when God would establish this covenant of peace. This was to be a much more comprehensive peace than simply an inward sense of peace.

As far as Paul was concerned, the promises of the prophets of old and the hope for a new covenant of peace were being realized in Jesus the Messiah. The age of God's new creation, God's promised kingdom, had broken in to the here and now. Because of what God had done through the death and resurrection of Christ, for Paul, the shalom of the new age—wholeness, well-being, justice, reconciliation, and harmony—had arrived. God in Christ, on the cross, has made peace with humanity and between humans.

So then, the Old Testament's covenant of peace has arrived, which for Paul meant that the new covenant community of Jesus-followers would be fundamentally peaceable in character, reflecting the Old Testament prophets, and, indeed, Jesus himself. The reconciliation that is at the heart of the gospel is not only about God and us; it's about how we reconcile with each other.

Peace is a central theme in Paul's letter to the Ephesians—the gospel, he says in 6:15, is "the gospel of peace." Paul explains that the state of hostility in which humanity exists towards God and each other has been negated by what God has done in Christ. "He came and proclaimed peace to you who were far off and peace to those who were near," Paul says, referring to the separation of Gentiles from Jews. Not only are people reconciled to God through Christ, they are to be reconciled to each other. Paul goes on to urge maintaining "the unity of the Spirit through the bond of peace" and that Jesus-followers clothe themselves with God's armor so as to be able to proclaim the gospel of peace—God's good news, which is essentially peaceful in character.

PAUL'S VIOLENT WORLD

But Paul's world was an incredibly violent one. Historians like Tacitus, Polybius, and Apuleius are all full of the brutality which characterized life in antiquity. The Roman military imposed the

so-called its *pax Romana* with extreme, gruesome violence—
"without restraint," says one historian. Banditry and piracy were
commonplace, as was violence between individuals at all levels in
society, including senators and Caesar's household.

Paul himself was a man of violence prior to his encounter with
the risen Christ. In Galatians 1:13, he talks about his former life
and how he "persecuted the church of God beyond measure and
tried to destroy it." The Greek here points to excessive force and
violence employed by Paul (of which he is now clearly ashamed).
But Paul turned away from this violent way of life and became a
follower of Jesus, whom all the early Christians remembered as a
proponent of peace and non-violence.

And what becomes evident from the history of the early
church and the New Testament is that, in following Jesus, the early
church lived in a quite different way from the world around.

PEACE AS A WAY OF LIFE

Jesus said, "Love your enemies." So, it's no surprise to hear Paul in
Romans and in other letters also talking about enemy love. But not
only is non-retaliation important for Paul, we find themes like reconciliation, peace, love, doing good, all occurring again and again.

Vengeance, cursing, and tallying up evils received can never
be on the table, according to Paul in Romans 12. On the opposite
side of the equation, Paul advocates doing good, blessing, concili-
ating, forgiving, and loving.

Evil and violence were all around these early Jesus-followers.
As is usually the case, it was the poor who disproportionately experienced violence in their lives, and it was no different for the
Roman Jesus-followers, not least those who were enslaved, who
often suffered cruel mistreatment, including whipping, branding,
and rape. But, says Paul, peace-making, doing the good, loving the
neighbour and enemy are the Christian response to evil.

Paul and his little Christian communities were often harassed, blamed for the ills that befell their communities, spoken ill

of and despised. But God, and Paul, called them—and us—to live in peace with everyone.

And more than that, to actively love our enemies.

PEACE AMONGST JESUS FOLLOWERS

And Paul was concerned that there be peace *within* the community of those who follow Jesus too. As we read Romans, Paul has a lot to say about the need for reconciliation between believers. From what we can tell from chapters 11, 14 and 15 of the letter, it looks like there were some tensions in Rome between believers from a pagan background and those from a Jewish background.

So, Paul warns Gentile Christians not to be arrogant towards their Jewish sisters and brothers; he tells the Romans that they are one body in Christ and points them towards generosity, service, and acts of mercy. He warns against "quarreling and jealousy" and seeks to resolve the differences between Roman Christians over diet and festivals.

As the letter proceeds, Paul talks more and more about the need for harmonious relations between believers. In chapter 12, he urges no one to think of themselves more highly than they ought to think; he then tells the Romans that they are one body in Christ and points them towards spiritual gifts like generosity, service, and acts of mercy. They were to "pursue what makes for peace." In chapter 13, he warns against "quarreling and jealousy" and then in 14 and 15 seeks to resolve the differences between believers over diet and festivals.

So, the thrust of the argument in the letter seems very much to be directed towards urging reconciliation and peace amongst Jesus-followers. Paul wanted these Roman believers to be in harmony, to be the new community of the covenant of peace that was promised by the prophets and brought about by the death and resurrection of Christ.

In this way they would demonstrate the radical nature of the gospel.

And history shows that in the centers of the early church, non-violence was taught as a core component of the gospel and in the first couple of centuries Christians generally felt their faith was incompatible with military service. These first Christians lived in a radically different way from the world around.

And like them, God calls us to the way of peace. First of all, away from any sort of discord and disunity with other brothers and sisters in the body of Christ. Sadly, we do hear of Christians arguing, sometimes with little kindness and grace, about all sorts of things, to the point of the fracturing of relationships—everything from petty disputes about the arrangement of the pews to points of doctrine to politics. Disagreement is inevitable, but Paul's words must govern all our engagements with each other: "As much as possible, and to the utmost of your ability, be at peace with everyone" (Rom 12:18).

One prime way which serves to disturb peace and unity between Christians is an attitude of self-righteousness—holding on fiercely to certain ideas or doctrines with a palpable lack of love; thinking we're better than others because we've got the right way of things, leading to lack of cooperation, disunity and, worse still, splits.

I came across this quotation from a pamphlet of the American Abolitionist Society in 1911, which sums this up:

> It is a strange kind of fire, the fire of self-righteousness, which gives us such pleasure by its warmth but does so little to banish the darkness.[2]

That's the thing about self-righteousness—it's strangely satisfying and comforting. But ultimately, it's destructive. Self-righteousness is far from Christ's kingdom of peace. We are called to radical love, radical forgiveness, radical forbearance. We cannot afford to indulge negative attitudes and actions towards other brothers and sisters.

2. White, "The Dark Tower" pamphlet.

BEING THE GOSPEL OF PEACE

And we are called to be the gospel of peace to a needy world.

The major theme of in Romans chapter 12 through to the early part of chapter 13 is how one is to respond to evil. This is of particular importance to the Roman believers, living as they did as vulnerable, poor members of an unregistered sect in the centre of the brutal Roman Empire. Evil and violence were all around them. But, says Paul, vengeance belongs only to God and Jesus-followers are to respond to evil in a completely different way.

Paul's words in Romans 12, "Bless those who persecute you, bless and do not curse them" directly recall Jesus's teaching in both Luke 6:28 and Matthew 5:44. His "Repay no one evil for evil" recalls Matthew 5:38—39, Matthew 5:39 and 43—44. Paul's take on the use of violence is in lock-step with Jesus's teaching and behaviour.

For Paul, the Christian communities were expected to be societies that were ordered quite differently from the violent world around them. This was because they were communities of the new age, communities of the new covenant of peace, enlivened by the spirit of the peace-producing Jesus.

To a normal way of thinking in Paul's world, talk of responding to violence peacefully and non-violently was insane. That's not how the world works! But it makes no more sense in our world, where our societies seem increasingly inclined to go to war to solve international problems. Over recent years we've seen an increasing glorification and near worship of the military. The military option, sadly, is often not the last resort; it's far too readily on the table when problems arise.

In his farewell address in 1961, President Eisenhower warned against the undue influence of what he called the military–industrial complex—an unholy alliance between the military and the defense industry that supplies it. Over the past 60 years, we've seen that influence over public policy continue to grow in the United States and other Western states, with a reverence for the military that is sacrosanct. A situation where churches celebrate war victories and the military would have been unthinkable to Paul and the first Christians.

We've developed a huge tolerance for violence, especially if it happens to people far away. We've swallowed the myth of redemptive violence. Our "way of life" is worth much more than the lives of the innocent men, women, and children who are the worst sufferers in our wars across the ocean.

And this is a huge challenge for us Jesus-followers: to free our minds from the dominant myth of violence that underpins our world; to resist the violence that is so pervasive—particularly that which is perpetrated on the most vulnerable: the unborn, the poor, immigrants, women. And to resist that using the weapon of love, rather than more violence.

God calls us to follow Jesus in the way of peace, of reconciliation, of forgiveness, as God in Christ has forgiven us.

We are called to live peaceably with God, with others, and with the entire creation. It's how we demonstrate the kingdom of God.

As Paul said in his letter to the Philippians: "practice these things, and the God of peace will be with you."

REFLECTION

What does the idea of shalom mean—for me, my family, our church family?

How big a problem is self-righteousness? What sort of problems have you seen it cause? Can you see it in your own life?

In what practical ways can we obey Jesus's command to love our enemies and Paul's injunction not to seek revenge?

In what ways do we see the "myth of redemptive violence" propagated in our daily lives?

It's been said that, after the first few centuries, Christians "made peace with war." Has that been true? Are our modern states too quick to resort to war?

FURTHER READING

Jeremy Gabrielson, *Paul's Non-Violent Gospel: The Theological Politics of Peace in Paul's Life and Letters*, Pickwick, 2013.

Willard Swartley, *Covenant of Peace: The Missing Peace in New Testament Theology and Ethics*, Grand Rapids: Eerdmans, 2006.

Michael Gorman, *Becoming the Gospel*, Eerdmans, 2015, chapters 5 & 6.

Walter Wink, "Facing the Myth of Redemptive Violence," (ekklesia.co.uk, 2014).

10

Remember the Poor

A SEA OF POVERTY

THE GOOD NEWS THAT God has entered our world to redeem and reclaim it has got to be good news for everybody. So, is it good news for the poor, those who are on the margins, who have largely been left behind? I've travelled to India on many occasions and have spent time in rural villages and in slum communities in major cities where there is desperate poverty, and people live precariously on the edge, where sickness, unemployment, and debt can tip them over into disaster.

For many of us, our lives are so far removed from any of that that it's hard to imagine that a large percentage of the world's population lives dangerously close to the World Bank's so-called international poverty line of $1.90 a day, and nearly half the world—nearly 4 billion people—lives on below $5.50 a day, a figure that has barely changed in three decades.

Around 13 percent of the world is chronically hungry—including children who become stunted physically and cognitively, whose education is marred, whose ability to ward off disease is seriously impaired, and whose chance of any sort of full life is just about non-existent. Poverty robs children of their future, making them grow old before their time and taking away the sort of life choices we think of as normal.

Think about it—around half the world struggles to have access to good schools, shelter, health care, electricity, and safe water.

And because of growing inequality, poverty is becoming more and more of an issue in wealthy countries as well. In the United States, over 40 million people live below the poverty threshold, according to Poverty USA, and, in 2016, over 12 percent of Americans were not able to feed themselves properly. In the UK, the Social Metrics Commission found that around 22 percent of people and 34 percent of children were living in poverty.

The truth is that those of us who are well-fed, housed, clothed, working, and entertained (probably everybody reading this), live on an island of plenty on a sea of poverty.

In such a world, can the gospel really be good news? And if it is, you'd expect to find something in Paul's writings about this, wouldn't you?

PAUL'S WORLD

The Mediterranean world of the first century in which Paul lived was very different from our own. Apart from a few well-off and political elites, almost everybody lived in poverty or near poverty. At least one in three people were slaves. A quarter of all children died before their tenth birthday and another 25 percent died before they were twenty-five. If you got sick, there was no real medicine, so chances were, you'd die. Sanitation was poor, the environment was dirty, and accommodation was crowded, with little privacy. Work for most people was menial and physically hard. It was a daily struggle just to survive.

Most of us can't imagine the perilous existence that was the lot of the majority of people in Paul's world. It was a world fraught with hazard for everyday people, with disease close at hand and the constant danger of fire sweeping through a neighborhood because of cooking on open fires. Death was ever present.

This was the world of the first Christians. It's very unlikely anyone following Jesus came from the elite classes of Roman society, so everyone was just about getting by, their lives blighted by the same conditions and problems, survival a struggle, and the death of family members and friends commonplace.

Life for them, like their neighbors, was tough, but can you imagine the additional pressures they were under because they were viewed as dishonouring the gods, giving allegiance only to Jesus the Messiah? This could mean considerable economic hardship for them, as neighbours refused to do business with them because of fear they were displeasing the gods, and potentially bringing down some disaster on their neighbourhood.

PAUL'S LIFE

What of Paul himself? In his letters to the Thessalonians and the Corinthians, Paul repeatedly speaks of engaging in arduous, physical labour. Acts maintains he was some sort of artisan, probably a "leather worker." His lifestyle—that of a wandering evangelist—meant that he couldn't properly establish his trade in one place, so earning a living was difficult.

In 1 Corinthians 4:11 Paul says, "To the present hour we are hungry and thirsty, we are poorly clothed and beaten and homeless," and in 2 Corinthians 11:27, he describes himself as "often without food." He was a man who spent his life in considerable poverty and the difficulties which arise from that. In fact, in 2 Corinthians 6, Paul describes himself as "poor . . . having nothing."

In short, Paul was in as difficult circumstances as the Christians in the small congregations he founded.

Given, then, what we know about Paul's life and that of the people in the little congregations of Jesus-followers in the cities of the Roman world, it should come as no surprise that Paul had an interest in the poor. And, given all we've discovered about Paul's gospel so far, with its focus on God coming to renew the world to bring justice and love and joy, it'd be amazing to find that Paul didn't believe that a concern for the poor was an integral part of the gospel.

Paul is usually thought of as a great theologian, a thinker, an evangelist, and over the centuries people have debated his great themes of justification by faith and salvation. What is not often highlighted is Paul's concern for the poor.

GOOD NEWS FOR THE POOR

The gospel, remember, is the good news that God has broken into the world to reclaim it under the Lordship of Christ, to bring a new day of justice and peace, a new day of renewed people and renewed world.

And remember, that in Acts, the very first Christians were sharing what they had "as any had need." They had a daily distribution of food to the poor widows, and "there was not a needy person among them," writes Luke, followed very closely by "great grace was upon them all."

And you just have to go to the book of James, the leader of the Jerusalem community of Jesus-followers, to get some sense of these first believers' view of the world, where the author is utterly scathing about the possibility of being a Jesus-follower and denying the poor. If you don't care for the poor, James said, your faith is dead—you don't have any faith.

And, as always, we have to consider Paul's Jewish background, where the God of the Hebrew scriptures stands out as the protector of the poor, and where Israelites were reminded again and again by their prophets that God required them to take care of the disadvantaged—widows, orphans, and the poor—and to strive for justice.

God, whom the Psalmist said "maintains the cause of the needy, and executes justice for the poor" (Psalm 140:12), said that God's people were to "share their food with the hungry and to provide shelter for homeless, oppressed people" (Isa 58:7), and that those who "trample the head of the poor into the dust of the earth, and push the afflicted out of the way. . .profane my holy name" (Amos 2:7).

And, of course, we remember Jesus's reply to John the Baptist about his own ministry in Matthew's gospel: "and the poor have good news preached to them." And that Jesus commenced his ministry in Luke's gospel by reading Isaiah's words in the synagogue, proclaiming that God had sent him to "proclaim good news to the poor."

In Jesus's world in Judaea and Galilee, many people lived in poverty, oppressed and marginalized by a systemic injustice that strongly favored those who controlled economic and political power. All this was indicative to Jesus of the destructive powers at work in the world that would be overthrown by the inbreaking, liberating, loving, and joyful kingdom of God.

So, time and time again in the description of Jesus's ministry, particularly in Luke's gospel, the poor are highlighted—remember, for example, Zacchaeus, whose salvation was proclaimed after he had given half his goods to the poor. Throughout Jesus's life, those who were of no account in the power structures of the day, were the very ones to whom he ministered, announcing the upside-down-ness of God's kingdom.

All of this was Paul's inheritance, so perhaps it should come as no surprise to find in Paul that concern for the poor and needy was an integral part of being a follower of Jesus.

REMEMBER THE POOR

In Galatians 2, Paul speaks of his encounter with the other apostles in Jerusalem, where they discussed the scope of the gospel. A point of controversy was whether Gentiles had to become Jewish in order to follow Jesus.

Paul, of course, was adamant that this was not the case. In the end, there was consensus, and James, John, and Peter agreed that Paul could take his Torah-free gospel to the Gentiles.

But in verse 10, Paul says. "Only, they asked us to remember the poor, the very thing I was eager to do." Now, isn't that remarkable? Here, at the conclusion of this major discussion about the very nature of the gospel, Paul thinks it important enough to mention this crucial part of the agreement—that he and Barnabas remember the poor.

Not that Paul needed any persuasion on this point. He says it was the very thing he was eager to do. James, John, Peter, Paul—all agreed that remembering the poor was an integral part of the gospel.

And when we read Paul's letters, it becomes clear that Paul expected concern for the needy to be a hallmark of the groups of Jesus-followers to which he wrote. We've mentioned already that the vast majority of people in the Roman Empire lived in poverty or near poverty. And how Jesus-followers loved and supported each other, forming new communities that testified to the radical love of God.

So, time and time again, we hear Paul urging these believers to care and support one another, to "live in love." Given the difficult lives of most of the people in the churches, it's clear that concern for the poor was high on Paul's agenda.

But not only did Paul think believers ought to care for one another, their love needed to spill out to the wider community:

- In Galatians 6, Paul says "as you have opportunity, do good to everyone." The phrase he uses here, "to do the good" was in regular use in Paul's world, referring to financial contributions in community life.

- In 1 Thessalonians 5, Paul says "encourage the faint-hearted, help the weak," the weak here including those who are economically vulnerable.

- In 1 Timothy 5, Paul refers to the community's support for needy widows; and in Titus 3, Jesus-followers are to devote themselves to good works in order to meet the needs around them.

- In Ephesians 4, we find Paul urging Jesus-followers to work so they have enough over to share with the needy.

- In Romans 12, Paul talks about "acts of mercy" and says the Romans need to contribute to the needs of their brothers and sisters, and then goes on to say that they are to "associate with the lowly."

So, again and again, along with all the numerous times that Paul urges Christians to "live in love," we find his letters peppered with concern for the poor and disadvantaged.

THE COLLECTION

One of the ways that Paul sought to make good on his promise to "remember the poor," was the money collection that he mentions on several occasions in his letters (1 and 2 Corinthians, Galatians, Romans). This was a project that was of enormous importance to Paul, carried out in the early 50s.

Basically, Paul knew of great need amongst Jesus-followers in Jerusalem—possibly as a result of famine—and he wanted his Gentile Christians to help. It looks like he drove this fund-raising for several years before eventually taking the money to Jerusalem.

In Romans we learn that he was worried that danger lay in this trip, and we know from Acts that he was right to be concerned, because he ended up being arrested on his return to Judaea.

This collection, then, shows just how important meeting the needs of the poor was to Paul and how far he was willing to risk his own life for the sake of it.

Also, what it shows is how generosity was a part of first century faith. Because the believers that Paul was collecting from were themselves not well off. How is it that those who are in need themselves are often much more generous than those of us blessed by so much?

I remember at times being utterly humbled in visiting people in marginalized communities in India. People who had very, very little, but brought me food and bottled Coke which they really couldn't afford, just in order to be hospitable.

We can't read Paul's letters without realizing that Paul was deeply concerned for the poor, and that his good news about the arrival of God's kingdom through Jesus meant that love and care were to be shared generously both within the Christian community and without.

This is not some social gospel—this is an integral part of the gospel.

Which is something that the church of Jesus Christ knew from its inception, and in the early centuries, Christians were recognized for the way in which they fed the hungry, cared for the sick and dying, and loved each other and their neighbors.

Tertullian, a Christian author from the second century, wrote, "It is our care of the helpless, our practice of loving kindness that brands us in the eyes of many of our opponents. "Only look," they say, "look how they love one another!""

And a second century biography of the North African bishop, Cyprian, records him as instructing his congregation that, "there is nothing remarkable in cherishing merely our own people," but that doing good extended to everyone, including enemies.

The history of this early period, including the Christian response to devastating epidemics which devastated the Roman Empire, striking down huge swaths of the populations of the cities, again disproportionately the poor, shows how deeply integrated care for the needy was with the idea of following Jesus.

There's much in the history of the church to criticize, but there have always been Christians who have served the poor and understood that radical love and a commitment to justice is an integral part of the gospel.

PROCLAIMING THE GOOD NEWS

So, we return to the question at the beginning of the chapter: is the gospel of Jesus Christ good news for the poor?

For Paul, it most certainly was. The love of God he'd experienced in Jesus and the justice that was integral to the proclamation of God's newly arriving kingdom meant that compassionate care for everyone was at the heart of these new Christian communities. The Roman world knew nothing of the love of deities for humanity, or of the idea that love for a god would be expressed through love for others, or that love ought to be extended beyond your family or close community.

This was a revolution—but a revolution of love, and it was love that extended to those who would have been thought of as unworthy of love, those at the bottom, at the margins. Love for the unloved, the poor, those in desperate need, was not an add-on in any way—it was part and parcel of this brand-new creation that God was making.

This, then, affected those who were poor in two ways—for those within the Christian communities who were all pretty much, by our modern standards, themselves poor, there was a loving community of people who supported and cared for each other in very practical ways. And for those around them in need, this group of people sought to let that care and love spill over in compassion.

And beyond this, there was the promise of the consummation of God's kingdom, when, as Mary realized, the powerful would be brought down from their thrones and the lowly uplifted, the hungry fed with good things, and the rich sent empty away.

So, good news for the poor? Yes, and the rapid spread of Christian faith in those early centuries firmly attests to this.

But what about us, two thousand years on? Can the gospel still be good news to the poor?

Most of us who live in affluent countries, even those of us who live modestly, are far from poor. Everything in our cultural context puts the focus on ourselves—our governments desperately want to preserve our "way of life" and grow our economies at all costs; advertising and the media urge us every moment of the day to focus on our own well-being and consumption; and the prevailing winds of culture toss us about on the seas of self-realization, self-actualization, and self-promotion.

In addition, false political narratives have succeeded in convincing us that those in poverty have no one to blame but themselves, blinding us to the systemic injustice that keeps things the way they are, and encouraging us to ignore the great need that exists.

On top of all that, we have ghastly perversions of the gospel which promise wealth and prosperity, and intensely privatized, spiritualized versions of faith which are suspicious of what they fear as a "social gospel."

Yet, while everything conspires to distract us from the full, revolutionary scope of the gospel, the world, as we have seen, is full of people in desperate need.

This brings a huge challenge to us Jesus-followers who are well fed, clothed, sheltered, and entertained. The question we face is: how does my life engage with the poor?

In what way are we "associating with the lowly"? How are we "contributing to the needs of the saints"? In what ways are we "doing good to everyone"? Because this is part of the DNA of the gospel. The gospel should be, and is, good news for the poor. But only if we open our hearts and let it.

And at a time like this, when brothers and sisters and others all around the world are in need, in some cases starving, in what ways can we become the gospel and "remember the poor"?

Because this is how we demonstrate to a needy world the reality of our faith and the radical nature of Christ's loving kingdom.

REFLECTION

How do you react to the statistics about the sheer number of people living in poverty in the world? In your country?

What difference does understanding the poverty level of Paul and the first Christians make to our understanding of Paul's letters?

Is the gospel really good news to the poor?

In what ways can we "associate with the lowly"?

In what ways can we "become the gospel" for those whose lives are blighted by poverty? As Jesus-followers, who is our neighbor, and where is our responsibility?

FURTHER READING

Bruce W. Longenecker, *Remember the Poor: Paul, Poverty, and the Greco-Roman World*, Eerdmans, 2010.

Rodney Stark, *The Rise of Christianity*, HarperOne, 1997, esp. Chapter 4, "Epidemics, Networks and Conversion."

Mae Elise Cannon, *Beyond Hashtag Activism: Comprehensive Justice in a Complicated Age*, InterVarsity Press, 2020.

11

The Antidote for Anxiety

WORRIED MINDS

GIVEN THE DIFFICULT CIRCUMSTANCES and uncertainties of life in which Paul and his fellow Jesus-followers lived and the poverty they endured, we ought not to be surprised that anxiety was a constant battle for them.

In Jesus's Sermon on the Mount, the term "worry" occurs six times. One of the definitions of the Greek word used for worry in this passage in Matthew's gospel is: "internal disturbance at the emotional and psychological level that disrupts life."

That's something we all know about, isn't it? We've all felt it at times, that internal churning, those dark thoughts about what might happen, running round and round in our heads to the point that we can hardly think about other things. We're all acquainted with anxiety and worry.

The people gathered around Jesus in Galilee, like most people in rural situations at that time—and, indeed, most people in the Roman Empire—lived in considerable hardship, most of them at, or near, subsistence level. For families where the main bread-winner was a tenant farmer or a day laborer, life was uncertain.

People were worried about debt, about earning enough money for the very basics of life, including food, about health, and about how they would cope if something unforeseen came along. That "internal disturbance that disrupts life" was at a high level.

So perhaps it's no surprise that in this sermon, Jesus mentions worry six times.

This sort of anxiety, caused by poverty, deprivation, violence, and injustice is, of course, the lot of a huge swath of humanity today. The poor of the world have good reason to be anxious.

The vast majority of the world lives life on the edge, with real worries about the basic necessities of life. Those whose lives are blighted by poverty have a host of real worries—about how to feed their children, how to clothe them properly and send them to school, about whether there will be any paid work available today, about the security of the roof over their heads.

My wife works with people living on the margins in slum communities and mountain villages in India. There you'll find people there with real worries. Like Kumla, a poor Dalit woman, in a Himalayan village, who had been abandoned by her husband, and, along with her four children, was evicted from their home. With the help of my wife's organization, Saphara, a new home was quickly built for the family, only for them to be threatened with eviction again shortly after, on a cold Christmas Eve. Thankfully the family was rescued from the situation and they were able to stay in their new home. But this difficult situation illustrates the precarious nature of life for those who are marginalized and have little power over their circumstances.

I'm a fan of American blues music, music that developed as a response to the oppression and suffering of the black community, especially in the Southern States, in the early decades of the twentieth century. And in the blues tradition, there's a lot of reference in the songs to "worried minds." All the uncertainties and worries that injustice and deprivation bring creates anxious minds, worried minds. In one old blues standard, *Trouble in Mind*, the singer contemplates a range of ways of taking his own life, such are the circumstances he finds himself in.

Poverty creates worried minds, whether you're a Galilean villager, an African American living in the Jim Crow South, or in a slum in Nairobi or Mumbai.

PAUL, THE PHILIPPIANS, AND ANXIETY

And it was the same for the people in the little communities that Paul founded throughout the first century Mediterranean world. Given the difficult circumstances that we've seen that Paul and the first Jesus-followers had to face—a world fraught with peril and death ever present—people had great cause to be anxious.

Can you imagine the worries that must have assailed people like Sabina, the freed slave, now a stone mason getting just occasional work, who could never be sure of getting the jobs she needed to make ends meet? Or Primus, the slave, who did the dirty work of stoking the fires for the master's baths, and whose very existence depended on not making a mistake in his work and thus displeasing the master who might beat him to within an inch of his life? Worried minds were a constant for Sabina, Primus, and the other Jesus-followers they met with.

But as well as the dangers that everyday life posed, Jesus-followers faced an additional hazard—opposition from their neighbors.

This first century world was one of superstition. People blamed their misfortune on having displeased this or that god, on the "evil eye," and so on, and did what they could to placate the gods by offering sacrifices and trying to keep on their right side.

When misfortune overtook you, you wondered why the gods had turned against you. Had you not offered the right amount of incense, visited the temple as much as you should have, or what? But then, it dawns on you—those people following that new Jewish cult down the road, they've stopped going to the temple altogether, they don't honour the gods. In fact, they actively displease the gods by speaking against them and saying there's no god but their Jesus.

So, to add to their already worried minds, Jesus-followers had to put up with the suspicion, and sometimes downright opposition, of their neighbors. This could mean considerable economic hardship for them, as people around them refused to do business with them, fuelled by suspicion that their displeasing of the gods could bring down some disaster on their neighborhood.

A few years ago, I was teaching a class in India and there were two young women who had recently become Christians. Their whole family, who had been Moslem, had moved from a town about 100 kilometres away because of problems that had arisen when the father had become a Christian. He had run a successful retail business, but when people found out he had become a Jesus-follower, his business dried up, and they were forced to leave. And that's the sort of economic difficulty that Christians in the first century faced.

We discover this when we read Paul's letter to the Christians at Philippi. In verses 28—30 of chapter one, Paul talks about the Christians' "opponents" and about their "struggle." He says, "God has granted you the privilege of not only believing in Christ but of suffering for him as well."

So, as well as the general difficulties these people who were living on the margins faced, there was opposition from their pagan neighbours.

We've thought already about Paul's life—the hardship, the hunger, the beatings he endured in his constant traveling. When he wrote his letter to the Philippians he was in prison, which was no picnic to say the least. Most cells were dark, unbearably cold, and with a sickening stench from the few toilets. His waking hours would have been miserable and sleeping difficult. He would have depended on friends to bring him food and water.

On top of that, Paul says he doesn't know how things are going to go for him—he may live or he may yet be executed.

Can you imagine how tough Paul's situation was? Where the hours dragged on interminably in miserable surroundings? And where he doesn't know from day to day whether he will face the executioner's sword?

DO NOT BE ANXIOUS

So here we have both Paul and the Philippians living in considerable hardship, with their very existence on a knife edge. All of which makes some verses in chapter 4 of Paul's letter all the more remarkable:

> Do not worry about anything, but in everything by prayer and supplication with thanksgiving let your requests be made known to God. And the peace of God, which surpasses all understanding, will guard your hearts and your minds in Christ Jesus.

Paul knew this little group of Jesus-followers was anxious. But he knew there was an antidote to their worried minds. And what he says to them is nothing short of . . . shocking, actually. For a man who's in prison, dependent on others to bring him his daily food and not knowing whether he would live or die, to say to a group of people facing opposition and uncertainty, "Do not be anxious, rejoice, and again I say, rejoice," sounds scarcely credible. Paul, what are you on? What are you talking about?

How can it be that Paul says to the Philippians—and to us, in whatever may be our difficulties and uncertainties—do not be anxious?

Although most of us don't live the uncertain lives that Paul and his fellow Jesus-followers lived, or have to cope with the precariousness that a life of poverty brings, life has a habit of springing surprises on us. Stuff happens. One minute we're going along fine, and the next we, or someone we love, are facing serious illness, or our marriage begins to stumble, or our children start making bad choices, or we lose our job. We worry.

The very natural human response to encountering the difficulties of life is to worry. To allow the internal psychological disturbance to build as we fret over the outcome and become anxious about the worst that might happen.

The funny thing too, is that we get anxious at times when there really is nothing tangible to worry about. We who are clothed, housed, warm, educated, healthy, able to work, entertained day and night—we, too, somehow have worried minds.

Some of this comes from the nexus of modern life in which we are all caught—our world revolves around the pursuit of power, money, and control, and, to a greater or lesser extent, that affects us all. If we live and engage in the modern world, we are continually bombarded with advertising and media that tells us we need this gadget, that car, this perfume, that holiday. All day long, our economically-driven society pushes and prods us towards consumption, all the time whispering, "you need it," "you have to have it." All of which creates a kind of permanent state of anxiety.

If we let the world squeeze us into that same old mold and we listen to the siren voices of "just a bigger house, just a new car, just another expensive holiday," then the anxiety of the age begins to seep in, as we strive for what we don't need, and what ultimately doesn't satisfy.

William Wordsworth's sonnet is even more true than when he wrote it 200 years ago:

> The world is too much with us; late and soon,
> Getting and spending, we lay waste our powers
> . . . We have given our hearts away, a sordid boon!

Anxiety, it seems, is built in to our endlessly striving, materialistic, success-driven culture.

Yet Paul says simply, "Do not be anxious." To the hard-pressed Philippians and to us, in our hectic, driven lives.

PAUL'S FOUR ANTIDOTES TO WORRY

What's Paul's answer to the worried mind?

First of all, he says, "let your gentleness be known to everyone." The word Paul uses here has the sense of being kind, gentle, forbearing, which is the opposite of the thrusting, pushing, self-promoting, and acquisitive attitude demanded in today's world. An approach to life that favors kindness and preference of others, generosity, and sharing can free us from the anxiety-inducing striving for more that threatens to enmesh us.

Bob Dylan hosted a radio show a while ago and one of the episodes focused on what he called the "holiday blues." When the cares of life threaten to get you down, Bob said, "You don't need Dr. Phil . . . you don't need me. Just go out and help someone more unfortunate than you." Bob suggests going to a soup kitchen, or a retirement home, "maybe even a prison" to find someone to be with and to bring some cheer to. "No matter how bad you have it, somebody got it worse."

Bob's spot on with this bit of advice—it's amazing how just taking your eyes and attention off yourself and your own problems, and starting to focus on the difficulties someone else has, suddenly makes your own situation look not so bad after all.

Then Paul says, "the Lord is near." Does Paul mean that there is no reason to be anxious because the Lord is coming again soon to put everything to rights, to make a new heaven and earth? Or does he mean that the Lord is right there beside us in the midst of our trials and uncertainties?

Actually, we probably don't have to choose, there's probably a bit of both in there. Paul certainly had a sense that Jesus would return to set up his kingdom. But there's also the sense of the twenty-third Psalm—even when we walk through a dark place, the Lord is right there with us, every step of the way. Jesus, who has been there and done that, said he'll never leave us or forsake us. He's right there, holding our hands. And Paul thinks that that is incredibly anxiety-busting.

It's what he himself was experiencing right there in that prison cell—despite the chains, the conditions he was in, despite the falseness of other believers who were undermining him, Paul is incredibly upbeat in this letter, talking about his own joy and about having learned how to be content with whatever he had. He knew the Lord who had appeared to him on the Damascus road, who had put his Spirit within and changed him from the inside out, was right there beside him in his dark prison cell.

Thirdly, Paul goes on to mention prayer—releasing our worries and problems to our loving heavenly father. We're to pray about everything, he says. Whether it's a huge threatening problem or something much less important—if it's disturbing us, making us anxious, then we are to bring it to God. Paul does not advocate simply pretending our anxiety isn't there. He wants us to be real about our situation and to deal with it. And a big part of that is by prayer.

Prayer is a mysterious thing—we can't explain the mechanics of it. But there's something very powerful about bringing our requests and our worries to God. Paul says the outcome is that "the peace of God, which surpasses all understanding, will guard your hearts and your minds in Christ Jesus." His friend, Peter, said something similar, "Cast all your care on him, for he cares for you." I like that. There's the sense of unloading, of taking a weight, giving it to God to carry and walking away free from the burden, knowing that our loving God has it in hand.

Ultimately, worry is just a waste of time—it doesn't change anything and it can be paralyzing. Dietrich Bonhoeffer, Lutheran pastor and anti-Nazi dissident, preached a sermon on fear, just as the Nazis were coming to power in Germany, addressing the worry people felt about what was happening in their country. He said,

> Fear fills us with loneliness, hopelessness, and desperation. It drives us to decisions and actions that undo us . . . pollutes our thinking, distorts our judgment, cripples our resilience to evil, dislodges our love, and casts a gloom over our hearts . . . Fear takes away a person's humanity. This is not what the creature made by God looks like.

Paul's antidote to our worried minds is prayer—bringing the worry to God and leaving it there.

The final thing Paul mentions, and it's just tucked away in the prayer exhortation, is thanksgiving. And that's incredibly important. Modern psychology tells us that gratitude improves our self-esteem, increases our energy, helps our immune system, increases our sleep quality, and enables us to cope better with stress. So, Paul knew what he was talking about. It's like the old hymn says, "count your blessings, name them one by one." And that's great advice, really. In our house, we try every day to rehearse three things we're thankful for, big or small. And, in the context of our relationship with God, the giver of all the good gifts we enjoy, that's a powerful thing to do.

Paul, writing from his prison cell—knew that God was right there with him and the Philippians, and that reality, combined with his thanksgiving and his prayers, would bring an incredible sense of peace. Peace is God's gift to us. "My peace," Jesus said, "I give to you ... don't let your heart be troubled." This is a peace that far surpasses anything to be found elsewhere in the world and it's God's wonderful gift to us when we decide to stop nursing our anxiety and start trusting him.

So here we are. Enmeshed in a fraught, anxious world of get-more, be-more, achieve-more.

Surrounded by anxiety-inducing reports on the TV, radio, digital sources, and social media. And the temptation is to fixate on all of that and let it induce fear and anxiety.

At times, the source of the fear is real—we face real difficulties and bad turns of events. Aside from any practical action we need to take, we need to hear Paul's incredible, outrageous statement in the face of the most dreadful circumstances:

> Don't be anxious about anything. Let your requests be made known to God. And the peace of God, which surpasses all understanding, will guard your hearts and your minds in Christ Jesus.

REFLECTION

How does the picture of the anxieties of the early Christians and those in today's world who live in poverty affect the way we see our own circumstances?

How does our consumer society induce anxiety in us?

What causes you anxiety and how do you typically respond?

Does watching too much news /consuming media make us more anxious?

How possible is it to bring our worry to God in prayer and then leave it there?

What is the role of thanksgiving in all of this?

How might Paul's instructions change how you handle anxiety?

FURTHER READING

Gary W. Burnett, *The Gospel According to the Blues*, Wipf and Stock, 2014, chapter 9.

12

Paul's Women Leaders

WOMAN IN THE FIRST CENTURY

IT WAS HUGELY IMPORTANT for Paul that the good news of Jesus the Messiah should be good news for everyone. God's gift of life, the new creation, was indiscriminate and broke down every human barrier. Paul's world was very hierarchical, and when he established communities of Jesus-followers, he had to make sure they understood the full impact of the gospel. Everybody, he told them, was the same in Christ, so these communities could no longer tolerate divisions based on: ethnicity—whether someone was a Jew or a Gentile; social and economic status—whether someone was a slave or free; or on gender—whether you were a man or woman.

In Paul's world, in both his native Judaism and more generally in the Hellenistic culture of the first century, women were very much second-class citizens. Misogyny was rife. Playwrights and philosophers denigrated women roundly—Euripides referred to women as "this creature of ruin," while Aristotle thought of a woman as "a deformed male." There were some exceptions, but women were generally treated as their husband's property, were not formally educated, and overall, not treated as full persons.

In Jewish tradition, there was generally a low view of women. The first century Jewish historian, Josephus, said that the woman was "in all things inferior to the man," and the Jewish philosopher, Philo, said that women were "imperfect and depraved by nature," irrational, and "not equal in honor with men." The second century Sirach said that "women give rise to shame," and the Testament of Reuben flatly states that "women are evil." In Jewish synagogues at this time, women were required simply to listen and forbidden to speak, and were not considered full participants in the assembly.

It was a man's world.

PAUL AND WOMEN

Today, it often seems as if people feel that Paul was not that much different from the culture in which he lived with regards to women. Some think that Paul's view of women is simply outdated and of no relevance to the modern world, where we all know that men and women are equal. We need to forget Paul. He's just sexist, maybe even misogynist.

For others, Paul gets held up as showing that only men should be teachers and leaders in the church. Whole denominations to this day still bar women from leadership. For some, men and women are just complementary and not equal, and men are the ones who are to have authority in marriages and in church.

But both these views of Paul misinterpret what we read in his letters and misunderstand the first century world. A careful reading of Paul's letters, actually, will lead us to a quite different conclusion.

Paul saw women and men as mutually dependent (1 Corinthians 11:11), as needing to submit to one another (Ephesians 5:21), and equal with respect to sexual relations within marriage (1 Corinthians 7:3). For Paul, all the gifts of the Spirit were available to everyone, regardless of gender, and everyone was to pursue spiritual gifts, especially prophecy, women as well as men. All Jesus-followers, female and male, were equally "in Christ," and were being transformed into Christ's image (2 Corinthians 3:18).

In addition, it is clear that Paul accepted women as ministry leaders. Women, as well as men, were his trusted partners and equals. He refers to women as "co-workers," as "contending at his side in the gospel," and as "true comrades." When we see Paul use these terms of women, as well as "deacon," "leader," "fellow worker in Christ Jesus," and, as we will shortly see, as "apostle," a picture of Paul emerges that is in stark contrast with the world in which he lived, and also with the way in which he is often portrayed today.

People who want to relegate women's roles in church usually point to two verses in 1 Corinthians and 1 Timothy which say that the women should keep silent in the churches and that a woman is not permitted to teach. Both these verses are usually plucked right out of their context and then flaunted as being the definitive view of Paul—and the Bible—on women in leadership. But, while it's important to take note of these verses, they are really not the place to start when we're thinking about Paul.

THE OLD TESTAMENT AND JESUS

It's important to remember again that Paul was a Jew and well aware of his Jewish scriptures, where we find wonderful woman leaders like Miriam, Israel's prophetic national leader and music director; Deborah, another prophet who led her country with great success at the time of the judges; and Huldah, whom King Josiah chose over all the male prophets. None of these, nor any of Israel's crowned queens, were ever criticized for their leadership roles on the grounds of being a woman.

Then we have the woman evangelist of Isaiah 40:9 who proclaims the good news of the coming of Yahweh's kingdom. The Hebrew here clearly identifies the preacher as a woman, all but lost in most of our English translations. Other women preachers are to the fore in Psalm 68:11: "The Lord announces the word, and the women who proclaim it are a mighty throng."

And, of course, we can't forget the prediction of the prophet Joel that God would pour out the Spirit so that "your daughters and sons will prophesy"—famously taken up by Peter in his sermon on the Day of Pentecost, when he was explaining what was happening to the crowd. And way that the Psalms and Isaiah and Hosea and Deuteronomy all describe God as a mother.

Despite the negative evaluation of women by his peers, Paul knew his Bible and was well aware of the strong tradition of women leaders, prophets, and preachers that was his heritage.

And he was taught by Gamaliel, who was greatly revered and honored by his own and successive generations. From what we know, Gamaliel was unlike other rabbis in Pharisaic Judaism, who had a very low view of women. In his sayings preserved in the Mishnah, Gamaliel affirms women, treating them equally with men, promoting their welfare, and is never derogatory about them—all this in contrast to other rabbinic teachers who, as we have seen, were positively misogynistic.

And Paul also had the example of Jesus, who, unlike other teachers of his day, allowed women to sit at his feet in the place of learning. Jesus welcomed women followers, and encounters with women like the Samaritan at the well, where he broke several social conventions, attest to his positive acceptance of women. There were countless women who were touched by his healing hands, including many who would have been considered ritually unclean. In addition, Jesus appeared first after his resurrection to Mary Magdalene, thereby showing his respect for a woman's testimony, over against the general prevailing culture at the time. And the gospel writers were prepared to identify women as the first witnesses of the resurrection, even though a woman's word in court was generally not acceptable.

No doubt all this contributed to the way in which Paul thought of women. What we read of Paul in Acts and in his letters reveals a Paul who was counter cultural and *radical* in his affirmative of women. As far as Paul was concerned, both men and women were equally redeemed in Christ, were one in the body of Christ, were equally priests in God's kingdom, had the Spirit poured out liberally on them equally, and were both humbly and lovingly to serve one another and the world. The broad thrust of his theology speaks volumes regarding the equality of woman and men in the church.

And, think of 1 Thessalonians 2:7, where Paul depicts himself as a nursing mother. Not what you would expect if Paul was your typical male chauvinist protecting a fragile male ego!

LET'S START WITH ROMANS 16

To find out what Paul thought about women in leadership, the place we need to start is his big letter to the Romans. And we need to go to chapter 16. Which I guess most of us have generally just skipped over—it seems to be just a bunch of names, people Paul is greeting.

But this is a very interesting chapter indeed. Paul has never been to Rome, so in this letter where he wants to gain the Romans' support for the mission he has in mind to Spain, he's careful here to greet the people who are the leaders of the Roman house churches.

The Roman church wasn't one big congregation; rather, it was a number of little groups that met in people's homes, often cramped tenement apartments. And we can tell a great deal from looking at the names in chapter 16—some are slave names, some are Jewish names, and some are Gentile names.

And some of them are women's names. People like Prisca, Tryphaina, Tryphosa, Mary, Persis, and Julia. All leaders or joint leaders of little congregations of believers in Rome. In fact, over two thirds of the colleagues whom Paul praises for their Christian ministry here are women. But there are three women who stand out.

PHOEBE

Firstly, Phoebe, who Paul says is a servant or deacon of the church which is at Cenchrea. Some translations have gone for deaconess—but there is no such word in Greek. When we look at the way Paul uses this word elsewhere, there really can be no doubt that

Phoebe is a leader in the church in Corinth, which is where Paul was when he wrote the letter.

Now when we look carefully at the language and words that Paul uses in verses 1 and 2, from what we know of letters in this period, Phoebe is a person of some standing, and she's a leader in the Corinthian church, entrusted with taking Paul's very important letter to Rome.

Now, the usual practice at this time was that the person who took the letter read it out and interpreted it to the recipients. Isn't that interesting? Paul's letter to Romans was hugely important to him—he had not been there, but wanted to gain the support of these Christians for taking the good news to the west of the empire, and so he is very careful to explain his understanding of the gospel. Whom does he entrust his letter to? To Phoebe, this senior woman leader, and she takes it to Rome.

It gets more interesting—because it's likely that, according to normal practice, when she got to Rome, Phoebe would have gone around the various house churches reading out the letter (remember, because of literacy issues, people would have heard, rather than read the letter), and then sat with the groups, making sure they understood what Paul was getting at.

We could imagine Paul sitting with Phoebe back in Corinth, taking her through the letter, telling her how he wanted it read, what he wanted to stress, and what bits she'd probably have to explain.

So Phoebe—a church leader, entrusted by the apostle with explaining and teaching his letter to the Romans—doesn't fit at all what we've been told Paul thinks about women leaders and teachers.

PRISCA

Prisca, or Priscilla as Luke calls her in Acts, was someone with whom Paul worked in the gospel, along with her husband, Aquila. Prisca is always mentioned before her husband, which was unusual in Greek and Hebrew culture, indicative of the significant, possibly more significant, role she played in the couple's ministry.

They are both—obviously including Prisca—highlighted by Luke as instructing Apollos, who became a major figure amongst the first followers of Jesus. So, already from Acts, we know that Prisca was a church leader and teacher, instructing men. By the time Paul wrote Romans, the pair had located in Rome and were leading a house church. Paul greets them warmly, again putting Prisca's name first.

JUNIA

But then there's Junia, who appears in verse 7.

> Greet Andronicus and Junia, my relatives who were in prison with me; they are prominent among the apostles, and they were in Christ before I was.

The older NIV and some translations give the name here as Junias, making out it was a man, but the name is Junia, which is a Latin feminine name, given to slaves or freedwomen. We have lots of examples of this woman's name from the literature of the time, and exactly none of a man's name, Junias.

Happily, there is no longer any argument about what the name is and the new NIV has changed to reading Junia. Junia was a woman, probably the wife of Andonicus.

The reason why, in the past, people tried to make Junia into a man were the words that follow where Paul says that this pair were "prominent among the apostles." So, in a male dominated church, the idea that a woman could be said to be an apostle didn't fit. So quite amazingly, if you look at the history of what happened, you'll find that male scholars literally changed the Greek to make what is clearly a woman's name to a male name, Junias. It's worth knowing a little of this history.

Biblical scholars use a composite text of the Greek New Testament—a version that is deemed most likely to reflect the original writing, after examining thousands of old manuscripts. In the Greek New Testament composite texts from the Reformation up until Nestle's edition of the Greek New Testament in 1927, the Junia of Romans 16 was a woman. But, at that point Nestle decided that the name had to be male and so suddenly "Junias" appeared and Junia became a footnote. Then fifty years later, the Greek text compiled by scholars dropped even the footnote. It was only in the 1990s that the correction was made and what all the early Greek manuscripts and scholars knew to be the case was made clear—Junia was a woman.

But even though everyone now agrees about this, there have been some who have been so uncomfortable about what Paul actually says in this verse—that Junia, a woman, was an apostle—that they have tried to change "prominent among the apostles" to "well known *to* the apostles." You get that in the ESV, for example.

But, "prominent *among* the apostles" was the meaning of the phrase to all the early church fathers, who spoke Greek and knew very well how to translate a word!

Here's what Chrysostom in the fourth century had to say:

> Even to be an apostle is great, but also to be prominent among them—consider how wonderful a song of honour that is. Glory be! How great the wisdom of this woman that she was even deemed worthy of the apostle's title.

Junia was a woman and she was an apostle, a senior leader in the church in Paul's day.

So, if that's the case, along with Phoebe, Prisca, and the other women church leaders in Romans 16, then the conclusion is inevitable—women played a full role, as well as men, in leadership and teaching roles in the first Christian groups. That being the case, any other texts that we might think, at first glance, contradict Romans 16 have to be considered in the light of it. This, along with the witness of Acts, is the place to start.

OTHER TEXTS

The two texts mentioned earlier in 1 Corinthians and 1 Timothy, then, begin to look like outliers, and there is much that could be said of the background to these verses that would make us draw back from making what Paul says here of universal application. It would be unusual for Bible-believing Christians to form a theological view simply based on two verses, without taking into consideration the strong witness of the rest of the New Testament. But, unfortunately, that is really what has happened.

If you'd like to look at this further, you'll find the most detailed examination of these two texts in Philip Payne's *Man and Woman: One in Christ*.

Briefly, Payne's meticulous examination of the text concludes that 1 Timothy 2: 8—15 needs to be read against Paul's purpose in the letter of countering false teaching which had greatly influenced some of the women in Ephesus, whose activities in spreading this needed to be curbed. Nothing in the passage supports "a universal prohibition of women teaching or having authority over men" or supports a view that "women are inherently unsuited to teach or exercise authority over men in spiritual or any other matters." Nor, he says, "does Paul universalize this particular prohibition for all churches and all times."[1]

His investigation of 1 Corinthians 14: 34—35 is even more painstaking, and, along with other conservative scholars, he concludes, from evidence in early Greek manuscripts, that these verses are likely a scribal addition and unlikely to have been part of Paul's original letter.

There are very good reasons, then, not to take these two texts as normative or in any way as representative of what Paul thought about women being teachers and leaders in the church.

---

1. Payne, *Man and Woman*, 444

WOMEN IN LEADERSHIP

There are other passages in Paul's letters that need to be examined, if we are to come to a more comprehensive view of what Paul thought about women in the church and in family relationships. We've simply been concerned to redress the male-dominated perspective that has been prevalent in the church that has distorted what Paul has to say about women in ministry, teaching, and leadership. The Romans 16 passage is crucial to keep in mind when reading anything that Paul has to say on the matter. 1 Corinthians 11 is important to bear in mind as well, where Paul assumes that women will be publicly prophesying in the church.

It begins to look like Paul's had a bad rap. It begins to look like women have been sorely mistreated over the centuries, and that the Christian church has missed out big time by not allowing women to follow a calling into Christian ministry.

Which is a stain on the history of the church. It's well past time for every Christian church, denomination, and group to make sure that women get the opportunity to play their full role as ministers of God's grace, word, and pastoral care.

We need to take seriously Paul's words: as far as he was concerned, there was neither slave nor free, Jew nor Greek, male nor female—we are all one in Christ. The division between male and female, along with the other two divisions Paul mentions here, is gone in the body of Christ. This is not just a comment on the fact that the spiritual standing of woman and men before God is the same—Paul's "for you are all one in Christ Jesus" in Galatians 3:18 has implications for the social reality of the Christian community. In a parallel verse in Colossians 3:11, it is clear from the verses before and after that Paul sees the overturning of these sorts of divisions as having a practical outworking in the community life of the church.

And this brings us back to the big themes of the gospel that we've been thinking about. In Jesus, God has come to rescue and renew his world, and to make us fully human. That means there are no social, class or caste divisions between us. Nor can there be any racial or ethnic divisions, because each one of us, redeemed by Christ, is free to love and serve God in the way that God has called us. And exactly the same applies to women and men.

Paul would beg to differ—strongly—with any approach that puts women down, discriminates against them and says, you can't do this or that in the church. That is just so much part of the old order. There is a new creation.

We humbly serve the Lord Christ together, woman and man, as God gives us grace and strength.

REFLECTION

What has your experience been of how women have been treated in churches you've been associated with?

Does the story of Junia from Romans 16 surprise you? What implications are there from Paul counting Junia as one of the apostles?

Do you think that what Acts and Romans 16 says about women in leadership positions ought to be more influential than the 1 Corinthians and 1 Timothy texts have been?

How can churches go about redressing the balance in terms of women and men in leadership?

FURTHER READING

Eldon Epp, *Junia: The First Woman Apostle*, Fortress, 2005.
Scot McKnight, *Junia Is Not Alone*, Patheos Press, Kindle Edition, 2011.
Philip Barton Payne, *Man and Woman, One in Christ*, Zondervan Academic, 2009.

13

Changing the World Together

THE GOSPEL IN COMMUNITY

As we've looked at various aspects of the gospel and tried to distil down to the essence of Paul's thinking, it's been clear that what God is doing in the world is greater than any one individual. We started off looking at God's love, which is what gripped Paul and energized him and propelled him throughout his life, and, wonderfully, that is something that each of us can experience and revel in. The benefits of Christ's death and resurrection are personally experienced, transformative, and meaningful.

But, as we've seen, God's coming into our world to redeem and transform it has wider implications. We've seen how God wants to transform the world and bring justice and peace, and how God wants the gospel to be good news to the poor in very practical ways. And, we've seen that Paul thinks that the natural outcome of individuals giving their allegiance to Jesus is that they live in peaceful, loving relationships with each other and with their neighbors and the wider world around.

All of which brings us round to thinking about the church. That's a word that means many things in our world—it's the building, it's the Sunday morning service, it's a denomination, it's an amorphous historical institution.

But Paul uses the word translated as church on many occasions and it simply means "assembly" or "gathering." It was a word that in the Greco-Roman world referred to the gathering of the citizens of a city for deliberation or voting, and in Paul's scriptures referred to the assembly of Israel, which had been chosen by God. So it was an appropriate one to use for these little congregations of Jesus-followers around the Mediterranean world, who were "citizens of heaven" and "called" by God to be God's "own possession." Paul had a sense that individual groups were churches, but also that these were part of a worldwide group of people who had given allegiance to the Lordship of Jesus.

Along the way so far, we've noted a few of Paul's seemingly outrageous statements. He has a few about the church. He says that God's plan is that through the church God's wisdom is to be made known to the spiritual powers in the heavenly places (Ephesians 3:10); that God's plan is that a holy and blameless church be presented to God, "in all her glory, having no spot or wrinkle or any such thing" (Ephesians 5:27); and that the very creation is waiting for the time when God's children will be fully revealed in all their God-given glory (Romans 8:19).

When we look at the church you and I know, that all looks like a tall order! There seems to be a mismatch between Paul's lofty ideals for the church and the way he thinks the church ought to be, and what it actually is at times. That's not an easy one to resolve, but I think as we look at what Paul has to say, we can find some encouragement and inspiration.

INDIVIDUALISM

Although Christ's death and resurrection affects each one of us personally and God's purposes include each one of us, we need to reckon with the fact that New Testament faith is never simply an individual thing—faith in Jesus is always within the context of a community of other Jesus-followers. That can be a tough thing for those of us living in Western countries to grasp, because of the individualism that grips our societies.

There's a famous country song that's been recording by many artists, which boasts that "Me and Jesus got a good thing going, me and Jesus got it all worked out . . . And we don't need anybody to tell us what it's all about." And you might remember the old children's hymn, *Jesus Bids Us Shine*, that contains the line, "you in your small corner and I in mine." Sadly, of late the gospel has become something very personalized, very individualized, very private. Like so much in life these days, faith has come to be all about me—my beliefs, my worship, my daily devotions, my preferences for church life.

The church has come to reflect the individualism that is dominant in modern liberal democracies, where the values of autonomy, self-actualization, and the cult of consumer choice are deeply embedded into all of life. In today's American-European cultures, individualism is in overdrive, with the independent and autonomous individual lionized at the expense of community and family. Today only half of Americans report having meaningful, face-to-face social interactions on a daily basis, and any community which exists is often simply online.

Yet, as the philosopher Spinoza has pointed out, we are all profoundly linked in countless ways we can hardly perceive, and seeking a kind of exclusive independence exacts a heavy toll on us in many ways. Human beings exist most happily, productively, and creatively in cooperative relationship with others.

That's because we were made in the image of God, who is three persons existing together in perfect relationship. To be in God's image, then, means that our lives are lovingly related to both God and to others. Although our modern world thinks of a person in terms of what's internal, and that we ought to go deep inside to find what's there and find our identity, God has made us to be persons in relationship, who are defined and fulfilled by those relationships.

Other non-Western cultures have something to teach us in this regard. In South Africa, the word Ubuntu describes a way of life where our dependence upon each other is recognized—"I am because we are." We are all connected and can only achieve for ourselves as we seek the growth and progress of others. Archbishop Desmond Tutu said that Ubuntu was about being generous, hospitable, friendly, caring, and compassionate. "You share what you have. It is to say, "My humanity is inextricably bound up in yours." We belong in a bundle of life."[1]

Our fast-paced, acquisitive, self-absorbed culture has largely forgotten this.

PAUL'S GRAND VISION

Paul, uninfluenced by our hyper-individualism, understood the way in which human relationships have been restored in Christ, and the role that this new, restored humanity has to play in God's new world. Hence the grand vision he has for the church which we see in his letter to the Ephesians.

Referring to the church as a holy temple, Paul says we are a "dwelling place for God." He says that the church is the means by which God shows his wisdom to the spiritual powers and that it is the "body" of Christ. Paul saw that God had done something remarkable in the world through the death and resurrection of the Messiah. God's rescue of fallen individuals had resulted in a group of people who were a demonstration of God's love and power. It was a group amongst whom God, through his Spirit, could live, and through whom God would be active in the world.

Paul's idea of the body of Christ, which he explores on several occasions, is all about individual members of that body being active in the world in a variety of ways. That's the grand vision—that this made-new group of people, which would experience the reality of God's very presence, would be God's eyes and hands and feet, reaching out to each other and to a needy world in blessing.

So, although Paul's words on one level sound a little grand, actually, what he has to say about the church is incredibly practical.

---

1. Tutu, "Mission and Philosophy."

As we've seen, the first groups of Jesus-followers were a mixed group of people from the lower rungs of society—from artisans to homeless people to slaves. People like Sabina and Primus. Unlike most of us who are pretty self-sufficient, they desperately needed each other for survival. They needed all the support they could get from each other, at the level of food, clothing, and shelter. In addition, in a world where healthcare was virtually non-existent, care for the sick and looking to God for healing was hugely important.

That's why, after all the grand things Paul has to say to the Ephesians about the church, he encourages them to "be kind to one another and tender hearted," and to "share with the one who has need."

Life was tough, so practical help was vital, and encouragement needed. Paul's idea of the church being the body of Christ in his letter to the Romans includes more "spiritual" activity like teaching and prophesying, but also includes things like giving and showing mercy. He goes on in Romans 12 to encourage "contributing to the needs of the saints" and offering hospitality. Paul also wanted the Christians to expect God to heal and work miracles (1 Corinthians 12: 9—10), vitally important in a situation where these Jesus-followers could not afford medical care, and where the medical care available was next to useless anyway.

Unlike anything else the Roman world knew, Christian faith necessitated this sort of mutual, practical, caring love. It all sprang from the great generosity of God. God's grace and love encompassed all those who had come to follow Christ—of necessity, that was to spill over into their common life together.

Not only was practical sharing and helping one another important, but so too was encouragement. When life is hard, your master has been beating you, or you haven't been able to find work that day, or your children are sick, words of comfort and reassurance that others are standing with you are hugely important. So the spiritual gifts Paul talks about in his letters included a variety of "speaking" gifts—prophecy, words of wisdom, and encouragement. Prophecy, he said was about speaking to others "for their upbuilding and encouragement and consolation" (1 Corinthians 14:3).

We can begin to see how Paul and his fellow Jesus-followers simply would not have understood a version of Christian faith that was just about "me and Jesus." They were all in it together—they had to be.

And together Paul saw them as demonstrating a different way of being human to the world, where they "shone like stars in the world." These little churches were beacons of light shining into the darkness of the Roman Empire, a foretaste of God's coming kingdom, showing forth the joy and vitality of communities of love and peace.

And, as we've seen already, the world around sat up and took notice, and the church experienced tremendous growth in those early centuries.

UNITY AND DIVERSITY

Was all rosy in these early Christian communities? Despite Paul's grand vision for what the church is and what it ought to be, he knew that community life could have its difficulties too. So, most of his letters were written in the knowledge of, and to address, problems that the churches in various locations were having.

In his letter to the Galatians, Paul has been disturbed by hearing about missionaries from a Jewish background disturbing the faith of the Gentile Jesus-followers in Galatia. A major point of controversy amongst the early Christians was whether someone from a pagan background needed to become Jewish and obey the Jewish Torah in order to follow Jesus. After all, Jesus was a Jewish Messiah, it was Israel's God at work in the world, and it was Jewish scriptures that had foretold it all. To many Jewish believers, it seemed logical that pagans needed to follow the Law—the men needed to be circumcised (ouch!), and everyone ought to follow Jewish dietary practices and observe Jewish festivals.

Paul would have none of this and insisted the gospel needed to be Torah-free, and that the only basis for being included in

God's people was allegiance to Jesus. So, Paul is not happy with the Jewish Christians from Jerusalem who have been misleading the Galatians and with the Galatians for listening to them. There is, he insists in Galatians 3:28, "neither Jew nor Greek" in Christ. Everyone is included simply on the basis of their relationship to Jesus.

This Jewish-Gentile strain pops up in other letters as well—notably Romans, where there were clearly tensions between the two groups, to judge by what Paul has to say in chapter 14 of the letter, where he talks about the "strong" and the "weak," two groups at odds over their attitudes to Jewish diets. In chapter 11, he has to remind the Gentile believers in Rome, who seem to be looking down their noses at their Jewish sisters and brothers, that it is they who have been grafted in to the ancient vine of God's people. And in the early part of the letter, Paul makes it very clear that both Jews and Gentiles are in the same boat with respect to being sinners, both equally in need of God's action in Christ, and both equally saved through Christ. Given that Paul was hoping for the support of the Roman house churches for his proposed mission to Spain (Romans 15:28), he wanted the believers there to be united, of one heart and soul.

This controversy, and Paul's desire that there needed to be unity and peace, shows just how difficult church life can be. Even in these early communities, where they needed to rely on one another in practical ways, sometimes for survival, and where they experienced a vital sense of the presence of God through the Holy Spirit, the old human tendency toward division reared its ugly head.

Church life can be a mixture of incredible love and support, and crazy, harmful division. Which is why Paul time and time again appeals in his letters for unity, for bearing with one another, and, as he puts it in his wonderful chapter on love in 1 Corinthians 13, showing the kind of love which "bears all things, believes all things, hopes all things, endures all things." Fine words, when intoned at a wedding, but in the nitty, gritty of church life, hugely challenging. And only possible with the help and power of the Holy Spirit.

Peace and reconciliation loom large in Paul's letters. We often think of these in purely personal terms—God has reconciled each of us to himself and has put his peace in our hearts. These ideas are much bigger than that to Paul. He sees peace and reconciliation as working itself out in relationships between diverse groups of people, making them into "one new person" in Christ (Ephesians 2:14—15).

The sort of divisions Paul had to contend with were not only those between Jews and Gentiles, but also between slaves and free persons. The Roman world was terribly stratified, very hierarchical, and the abominable practice of slavery was part of life (and nobody, not even Paul, could imagine a world that was different, although, just maybe the sense that he did slips through in his letter to Philemon). People at every level of society treated those below them with little respect, and slaves with no respect at all. In addition, it was very much a man's world, where women had very restricted roles. Imagine in such a world an alternative society where everyone was deemed equal—equally sinful, yes, but equally redeemed in Christ, and treated equally and lovingly in the community. Masters and slaves, artisans and day-laborers meeting together to share the bread and the wine, sharing a "holy kiss." It was unheard of.

But that was the very nature of the gospel. And of the church.

TWO THOUSAND YEARS ON

And here we are, Jesus-followers twenty centuries on, living in a world full of division. Although our world has become much more egalitarian in many respects, we are divided in so many ways. The gap between the rich and the poor has risen to unprecedented levels; woman are still treated abominably in many countries and even in American-European cultures lag behind men in many respects; racism continues to be a scourge; attitudes to immigrants divide us; there is increasing political polarization, fuelled by instant communications and social media; and religious fundamentalism tears people apart.

All this can be a problem for the church. Or, it can be an opportunity. In a world rent by division, the church of Jesus Christ has a golden opportunity to demonstrate the healing, reconciling love of God. To form loving communities of people from diverse backgrounds who are willing to share generously with one another, in the knowledge that we are all one in Christ Jesus.

There is, of course, room for doing things in different ways, seeing things from a different perspective, organizing our communities differently. But Jesus-followers must first and foremost seek to follow the way of peace, of seeking reconciliation with those we might formally have been estranged from, and to cooperate with each other for our mutual benefit and the benefit of the world.

In my part of the world, Christians from Catholic and Protestant backgrounds were ignorant of each other, suspicious of each other, and actively opposed to each other for far too long. That has diminished a great deal, with some wonderful work accomplished together, but there is more to be done. But almost everywhere you look, you see would-be Jesus-followers prepared to allow the divisions of the world around to fracture their fellowship. The racism and segregation that has been a feature of church life in the United States, for example, is an affront to the gospel.

Paul's response would be in words he uses often in his letters—may it never be!

We need to pay attention to his words to the Ephesians, when he begs church members to "walk . . . with all humility and gentleness, with patience, showing tolerance for one another in love, being diligent to preserve the unity of the Spirit in the bond of peace" (Ephesians 4:1—3).

Perhaps the most concise—and beautiful—description of the church is found in the third chapter of Paul's letter to the Colossians. It comes right after saying that all human divisions are dissolved in the new creation that God has made—Jews, Greeks, barbarians, and slaves are all on an equal footing. Even Scythians, known for their excessive brutality and uncouth ways, were to be made right at home in the Jesus family.

As God's chosen ones, holy and beloved, clothe yourselves with compassion, kindness, humility, meekness, and patience. Bear with one another and, if anyone has a complaint against another, forgive each other; just as the Lord has forgiven you, so you also must forgive. Above all, clothe yourselves with love, which binds everything together in perfect harmony. And let the peace of Christ rule in your hearts, to which indeed you were called in the one body. And be thankful. Let the word of Christ dwell in you richly; teach and admonish one another in all wisdom; and with gratitude in your hearts sing psalms, hymns, and spiritual songs to God. And whatever you do, in word or deed, do everything in the name of the Lord Jesus, giving thanks to God the Father through him.

There you have it—compassion, kindness, forgiveness, thankfulness, and worship. That's what the church of Jesus Christ is to look like.

THE CHURCH AND THE WORLD

William Temple, a twentieth century Archbishop of Canterbury, famously said that "the Church is the only organisation that does not exist for itself, but for those who live outside of it." Paul would have wholeheartedly agreed.

We've already looked at the implications of the good news of Jesus the Messiah for bringing peace and justice to the world, and the way in which the gospel is good news for the poor. Paul wanted everyone to come to "the obedience of faith," and expected the love and mutual care experienced within his communities to overflow to the world around. Clearly these early believers were keen to tell their neighbors what God had done through Christ, but from what we know of early church history, it was the sustained expressions of love to sick, poor, and disabled neighbors, even in the midst of terrible epidemics, that brought large numbers of people into the Christian family.

Christians did indeed shine like stars in the world, and as they "lived in love," their neighbors noticed and many were attracted. At times, of course, the message of the arrival of a new king was received badly by the authorities and Christians were persecuted for their allegiance to Jesus.

And here is the challenge for us. For us who live in parts of the world where our individual rights, perceived needs, comfort, and preferences take priority, who feel we have little need of others—where hyper-individualism rules and divides us and makes false promises to us.

Our faith—and our lives—can never be fully realized on our own. Just me and Jesus will never cut it. We need each other. We need the encouragement, the support, and the challenge that only sharing our lives with others will bring. We need to be part of the church.

And, more than that, the world needs to see groups of Jesus-followers that proclaim the reality of the kingdom of God, through their shared joy, worship, and overflowing love. And their willingness to stand up for justice and give a voice to those who have little or no voice.

Love is the essence and that means more than just an individual communing with God. Love means experiencing God's love through the kindness and encouragement of others, and loving God in return by means of the love we show to other sisters and brothers in Christ, our neighbors, and the wider world.

We'd be foolish not to recognize the flawed nature of the church and the fact that when you put a group of people together there is always the potential for problems. But somehow, in this imperfect collection of Jesus-followers, there is also the potential to change the world.

As we work together, support one another, love one another sacrificially, and express the love and justice and peace of the good news, we truly can be the body of Christ at work in the world.

REFLECTION

What has your experience of church been like? Remembering Paul's words about "forgiving one another as God in Christ has forgiven you," are there those you need to forgive? Are there those whose forgiveness you need to seek?

Leaving aside questions of organization, in the light of this chapter, what is the church? What is the essence of what the church is all about?

Has my experience of Christian faith been too individualistic? Do I need to invest more in relationships with other Jesus-followers?

In what practical ways can we seek to serve, support and encourage others in our church community?

How aware are we of the worldwide church? In what ways can we partner and show solidarity with brothers and sisters in other parts of the world?

How can the community of which you are a part better demonstrate the reconciling love of God to the world around?

FURTHER READING

Douglas A. Campbell, *Paul: An Apostle's Journey*, Eerdmans, 2018, chapter 5.
Susan Grove Eastman, "What did Paul think God was doing in Christian communities?" in Bruce W. Longenecker (ed.), *The New Cambridge Companion to St. Paul*, CUP, 2020.

14

Bringing It All Back Home

BOB DYLAN'S 1965 *BRINGING It All Back Home* album features a fallout shelter sign on a table, indicative, as it turned out, of the explosive nature of the album, where Dylan went electric and effectively redefined the nature of the pop song. It was an artistic leap that was the cultural equivalent of the nuclear bomb.

We might say something similar about the theology of the apostle Paul. His reimagining of his Jewish history and tradition in the light of the coming of Christ was an atomic bomb of thought that is still rippling through the world, twenty centuries later. I'm hoping something of the explosive nature of what he had to say has come through as you've read *Paul Distilled*.

I hope by now you have a better appreciation of Paul the apostle and can understand the debt we owe him for the way in which he thought deeply about the meaning of the incarnation, death, and resurrection of Jesus the Messiah, wrestling with his Jewish scriptures, listening to the Holy Spirit, and trying to see how it all applied in the day-to-day life of the little Jesus communities dotted around the Mediterranean world of the first century. And are beginning to see how this both sowed the seeds for what turned out to be a revolution in the empire over the next few centuries and has continuing importance for our lives as Jesus-followers and the life of our world.

Paul had his faults, of course—he had a sharp disagreement with Barnabas, his co-worker, which led to them part company; we can hear his sharp tongue when he refers to the Jerusalem leaders in Galatians 2, and his wish for circumcision preachers to go and castrate themselves later on in the letter; and he was clearly something of a driven man. During his life he was detested by various groups of pagans, Jews and Christians, some of whom wanted to kill him and at whose hands he was cruelly beaten and periodically imprisoned.

Paul did, however, recognize his faults, confessing to the Philippians that he was not perfect and needed to "know Christ and the power of his resurrection."

But he was a remarkable man, traveling around 10,000 miles during his lifetime, much of it by foot, spreading the good news about Jesus and seeking to establish communities of the new creation. In his mid-fifties—by the standards of his time, pretty old—far from settling down, he decided he needed a new challenge and wanted to start an entirely new mission in the west of the empire, going to Spain, where the gospel had not yet reached. His energy, determination and indomitable spirit were remarkable.

What drove him on, through hunger, shipwreck, torture, and opposition of various kinds?

Three things, I think, stand out, as we have seen, as we've tried to distil down Paul's thought. First, an experience of the love of God. He had personally encountered the living Jesus, the "Son of God, who loved me and gave himself for me." Paul was a man who, in his former life had known hate and violence—he had viciously attacked the new sect of Jewish Jesus followers, trying to stamp it out completely.

But, amazingly, miraculously, when he was on his way to perpetrate more brutality, Paul came face-to-face with the risen Lord Jesus, and came to understand the reality of what God had done through his life, death and resurrection. It was in this way that God's plan to redeem and to save humanity, lost and estranged from him, had been worked out, and, above everything else, this was a mind-shattering demonstration of love. God, he told the Roman believers, had uniquely and supremely shown "his love for us in that while we still were sinners Christ died for us."

Paul knew that to be true from his own experience of God's love and mercy. He didn't mind admitting that he had been "the worst of sinners," and he knew that at the centre of this cataclysmic event of God's breaking into the world through the Messiah Jesus was God's all-encompassing love for humanity. He knew that God had forgiven him, given him his Spirit, and was right there with him in every difficult circumstance of his life.

And he was convinced that the way in which to respond to this incredibly loving God was to love God back—but that this would be done primarily by loving other people. As God's love to us is indiscriminate and lavish, so too is our reciprocal love to be, as shown to others.

Secondly, Paul's encounter with the risen Jesus had left an indelible mark on him. This convinced him that the world had changed dramatically. Everything rose or fell on this one fact of Jesus's bodily resurrection. As he searched his scriptures and tried to make sense of this, he realized that Jesus was now Lord of all, and that every power that held people captive, and everything that conspired to cause people to live inauthentic human lives, was utterly defeated.

This included the ultimate power of death. The resurrection of Jesus meant that Jesus-followers, now counted as "in the Messiah" would also be resurrected, that death was not the end for them. Rather, they would rise to be part of God's newly restored, sin-free, just, peaceful world. Jesus's resurrection meant resurrection for Jesus-followers, something that would be fully realized in the consummation of God's new kingdom, but was already a reality in the minds and lives of those who owned allegiance to Jesus. They were already new people, able to live in a way that was radically different from the world around.

Jesus's Lordship also meant that God has come to reclaim his world, and that God's new world of justice and peace has broken into the present in the lives of Jesus-followers. As they submit to King Jesus and say no to the injustice, violence, and self-centeredness of the world, they are to demonstrate and model the reality of God's coming kingdom of justice, peace, and joy.

Thirdly, all of this was made possible by the power of the Holy Spirit, which fills Jesus-followers with the presence of God, and enables them to live in a dramatically different way from the world around. Paul saw the Spirit at work in the worship of the Jesus communities, as they encouraged and supported each other through the gifts the Spirit bestowed on them, and in the way the Spirit enabled believers to support one another in the tough lives they lived, through practical action which embodied exceptional love and compassion.

God's love; the death and resurrection of Christ; the Lordship of Jesus; the power of the Holy Spirit. All of this thought through and applied to the circumstances of the congregations to which he wrote. It's interesting to work through what Paul has to say against the historical background of his life and the first Jesus-followers in the middle of the first century. But we really want to know what it means for us. The so what? question.

After the fall of communism in 1991, political scientist Frances Fukiyama hailed the triumph of liberal democracy as "the end of history." Thirty years on, with inequality rampant in America and Europe, the fissures in society because of long-simmering racism becoming very apparent in the United States, the demise of truth in the public square, economic uncertainty, and the rise of utterly self-interested national leadership, Paul's message of love and the Lordship of Christ is as urgent as ever. Add in the rising poverty and hunger in the developing world and the global effects of the pandemic, and you've a world desperately in need of Jesus-followers to "shine like stars."

To do that, as Paul counselled the Philippians, we need to "have the same attitude as that in Jesus the Messiah," i.e., a willingness to take on Christ's humility, to "look not just to our own interests but the interests of others." If Jesus-followers everywhere were to take this seriously, it would have a massive effect on the world. What would be the effect if we:

- Let the love of God surround us and fill us to dispel our anxieties and self-absorption, to set us free to live in love and joy

- Rejected the consumerist urges that we almost unwittingly submit to every day and invested our resources in helping others

- Ensured we spent enough time with our families, communities and the wider world, rather than working incessantly

- Took seriously Paul's sense that the gospel requires us to "remember the poor"

- Like Paul's communities and the rest of the communities of Jesus-followers in the first century, were radically committed to not taking revenge, and to non-violence and peace

- Found ways of standing in solidarity with those who suffer from racism, and, like the first Christians, formed multi-ethnic, multi-racial communities of love

- Embraced a radical faithfulness in all our relationships

- Embraced an equality between men and women, including leadership, and rejected all forms of sexism.

How invested are we, as Jesus-followers, in the status quo, as opposed to the radical kingdom of God? What Paul has to say brings tremendous challenges to us who are well-fed, sheltered, at least relatively well-off, and entertained. Will we bow the knee to King Jesus, reject the radical individualism of our modern world, and seek to "live in love"?

There's no promise of prosperity and a life of ease in Paul's gospel. But there is the prospect of unparalleled joy, the vibrant life and power of the Holy Spirit, and the support of other brothers and sisters as we live the resurrection life. We can, indeed, be more than conquerors, through him who loved us. And in the end, even that last, old enemy, death itself, won't hold us back from the new world that God will make. Nothing can separate us from the love of God.

> Now to him who by the power at work within us is able to accomplish abundantly far more than all we can ask or imagine, to him be glory in the church and in Christ Jesus to all generations, forever and ever. Amen. (Ephesians 3:20—21)

Thanks

To CHRISTINE FOR HER unfailing love, support and wisdom; to Paddy, for his friendship over so many years and for reading the manuscript so thoughtfully; to Ian for his encouragement and friendship; to Rev. Steve and Pastor Paul for their support for this project; and to the many New Testament scholars from whose work I've benefited over many years.

Bibliography

Brueggemann, Walter, *Interpretation and Obedience*, Minneapolis: Fortress, 1991.

Burnett, Gary W., *The Gospel According to the Blues*, Eugene: Cascade, 2014.

Cannon, Mae Elise, *Beyond Hashtag Activism: Comprehensive Justice in a Complicated Age*, Westmont: InterVarsity Press, 2020.

Campbell, Douglas A., *Paul: An Apostle's Journey*, Grand Rapids: Eerdmans, 2018.

———. *Pauline Dogmatics, The Triumph of God's Love*, Grand Rapids: Eerdmans, 2020.

Dunn, J.D.G. & Suggate, Alan M., *The Justice of God: A Fresh Look at the Old Doctrine of Justification by Faith*, Grand Rapids: Eerdmans, 1994.

Eastman, Susan Grove, "What did Paul think God was doing in Christian communities?" In *The New Cambridge Companion to St. Paul*, edited by Bruce L. Longenecker, 210–224. Cambridge: CUP, 2020.

Epp, Eldon, *Junia: The First Woman Apostle*, Minneapolis: Fortress, 2005.

Fee, Gordon D., *God's Empowering Presence: The Holy Spirit in the Letters of Paul*, Peabody: Hendrickson, 1994.

———. *Paul, the Spirit and the People of God*, Peabody: Hendrickson, 1994.

Gabrielson, Jeremy, *Paul's Non-Violent Gospel: The Theological Politics of Peace in Paul's Life and Letters*, Eugene: Pickwick, 2013.

Gorman, Michael J., *The Death of the Messiah and the Birth of the New Covenant*, Eugene: Cascade, 2014.

———. *Participating in Christ: Explorations in Paul's Theology and Spirituality*, Grand Rapids: Baker, 2019.

Kirk, J.R. Daniel, *Unlocking Romans: Resurrection and the Justification of God*, Grand Rapids: Eerdmans, 2008.

Longenecker, Bruce L., *Remember the Poor: Paul, Poverty, and the Greco-Roman World*, Grand Rapids: Eerdmans, 2010.

———. "What did Paul think was wrong in God's world?" In *The New Cambridge Companion to St. Paul*, edited by Bruce L. Longenecker, 171–186. Cambridge: CUP, 2020.

Levison, John R., *Fresh Air: The Holy Spirit for an Inspired Life*, Orleans, Ma.: Paraclete Press, 2012.

Mitchel, Patrick, *The Message of Love: The Only Thing that Counts*, London: Inter-Varsity Press, 2019.

Peter Oakes, *Reading Romans in Pompeii: Paul's Letter at Ground Level*, London: SPCK, 2009.

McKnight, Scot, *Junia Is Not Alone*, Patheos Press, Kindle Edition, 2011.

———. *The King Jesus Gospel*, Grand Rapids: Zondervan, 2011.

Payne, Philip Barton, *Man and Woman, One in Christ*, Grand Rapids: Zondervan Academic, 2009.

Stark, Rodney *The Rise of Christianity*, New York: HarperOne, 1997.

Tutu, Desmond, "Mission and Philosophy," (http://www.tutufoundationusa.org/desmond-tutu-peace-foundation/).

White, Augustin Craig, "The Dark Tower", a pamphlet of the American Abolitionist Society, 1911.

Willard, *Covenant of Peace: The Missing Peace in New Testament Theology and Ethics*, Grand Rapids: Eerdmans, 2006.

Wink, Walter, "Facing the Myth of Redemptive Violence," (ekklesia.co.uk, 2014).

———. *Naming the Powers: The Language of Power in the New Testament*, Minneapolis: Fortress, 1984.

Wright, N.T., *Evil and the Justice of God*, London; SPCK, 2006.

———. "On becoming the righteousness of God," in D.M. Hay (ed.), *Pauline Theology, Volume II*, Minneapolis: Fortress, 1993.

———. *The Resurrection of the Son of God*, London: SPCK, 2003.

Wright, Tom, *Surprised by Hope*, London: SPCK, 2008.

———. *What Saint Paul Really Said*, Oxford: Lion Books, 1997.

Wolterstorff, Nicholas, *Justice in Love*, Grand Rapids: Eerdmans, 2011.

Lightning Source UK Ltd.
Milton Keynes UK
UKHW021150061221
395181UK00006B/289